The ROAD to RECOVERY

Russell

The ROAD *to* RECOVERY

Bridges between the Bible
and the Twelve Steps

DENNIS C. MORREIM

Foreword by John E. Keller

Augsburg ▪ Minneapolis

THE ROAD TO RECOVERY
Bridges between the Bible and the Twelve Steps

Cover design: Lecy Design

Library of Congress Cataloging-in-Publication Data

Morreim, Dennis C., 1942–
    The road to recovery : bridges between the Bible and the twelve
steps / Dennis C. Morreim ; foreword by John E. Keller.
        p.   cm.
    Includes bibliographical references.
    ISBN 0-8066-2456-6
    1. Alcoholics—Religious life. 2. Alcoholics Anonymous.
3. Twelve steps and twelve traditions. 4. Self-help groups.
5. Alcoholism—Religious aspects—Christianity. 6. Substance abuse—
Religious aspects—Christianity. 7. Co-dependence—Religious
aspects—Christianity. I. Title. II. Title: Bible and the twelve
steps. III. Title: Twelve steps.
BV4596.A48M67   1990
248.8'6—dc20   89-49091
                                                                   CIP

The paper used in this publication meets the minimum requirements of American National Standard for Information Sciences—Permanence of Paper for Printed Library Materials, ANSI Z329.48-1984.   ∞™

Manufactured in the U.S.A.   AF 9-2456

99   98   97   96   95   4   5   6   7   8   9   10   11   12   13

To my father and mother

Contents

Foreword

In the late 1950s a group of recovering alcoholics in Alcoholics Anonymous who were raised in the church, some not yet having returned to the church, expressed an interest in what Dennis Morreim describes as "bridges." Some were looking for bridges to a more meaningful understanding and experience of the Christian faith in relationship to the AA fellowship and spiritual recovery program. Others were looking for some bridges to enable their return to the church.

When I read Dennis Morreim's manuscript, I thought of that group and felt that this book could have been very helpful. It was also gratifying to know that this book was written by a parish pastor who has been interested and involved with alcoholics rather than by a professional in the field.

Morreim's awareness of and sensitivity to AA not being a religion, of AA and the Christian church being "two different roads," are key in this book. He neither seeks to make AA into the Christian religion nor to make the Christian church the equivalent of AA. He knows that there can be no affiliation but that there are bridges between the two. The church can and needs to hear from AA. The church also has a message that addresses needs outside and beyond the nature and scope of AA.

A recovering alcoholic active in AA but not in the Christian church can read this book and remain outside the church without a sense of being a lesser person. On the other hand, if he or she has an interest in taking a closer look at the church's message, this book will be helpful. The choice and placement of "bridges" and Scripture texts provide bridges from the language in the AA program to the language of the Bible.

The first pastor involved with founder Bill Wilson in connection with what became AA was Dr. Samuel Shoemaker, an Episcopalian priest. In introducing Shoemaker to the Twentieth Anniversary Convention of AA in St. Louis in 1955, Wilson said, "It is through Dr. Shoemaker that most of A.A.'s spiritual principles have come. He has been the connecting link."[1]

In his address Shoemaker said:

> None can doubt that God is what has made A.A. what it is today, what inspires it, what keeps it going, what is that perfectly intangible but unmistakable spirit that we have felt again and again since we have been here in St. Louis. I am thankful that the Church has so widely associated itself with A.A., because I think A.A. people need the Church for personal stabilization and growth, but also because I believe the Church needs A.A. as a continuous spur to greater aliveness and expectation and power. They are meant to complement and supplement each other.[2]

Dennis Morreim believes Shoemaker's statement. This book identifies and describes some "bridges" that recovering alcoholics in AA can cross to experience in more meaningful ways the Christian religion within the community of faith.

JOHN E. KELLER

Preface

This book comes out of struggle. It comes out of my own personal struggle to bridge the gap between what I have heard taught in the Twelve Steps of Alcoholics Anonymous and what is taught and preached in the church. It also comes out of listening to many recovering people, either in personal conversations or during "fifth steps," who wrestle with how they are going to fit into their lives what they hear in the Twelve Steps and what they hear in church.

Some to whom I listen express a desire to return to church but are apprehensive, wondering if what they will hear there will help or hinder their recovery. They worry, Are the two compatible? Will one of these life-giving communities have to be left behind?

How does one bridge these two life journeys, AA and the church? I believe there is one common source upon which bridges can be built: the Bible.

This is a book, then, about bridges. It is about the Twelve Steps. It is about the Bible. If you are in a Twelve-Step program or are familiar with one, it is my hope that these bridges between the steps and the Bible will be helpful to your spiritual journey. Even though I have written primarily for those in the Twelve Steps of AA, I believe these same bridges arch from the Bible over into any Twelve-Step recovery program.

The research found in this book comes from more than 50 taped interviews with recovering persons in AA, chemical dependency counselors, and pastors working in treatment settings. You will find excerpts from these interviews scattered throughout the book. All of those interviewed have some knowledge of or tie with the Christian faith. Some are active in the church, some are not, but they all have either a past or present experience with a church. Many of these people I have come to know very well; others momentarily crossed my path in life and gave me the opportunity to speak with them in depth. My questions to these people focused on the "bridges" (as I call them) they saw between the Twelve Steps and the Christian faith. Unfortunately a lack of space prohibits me from sharing all of what they said.

Passages of Scripture quoted are from the New International Version unless otherwise indicated. Regarding AA publications, I refer to the book *Alcoholics Anonymous* as the "Big Book," which it is commonly called. I also refer to the book *Twelve Steps and Twelve Traditions* as the "12 X 12."

Acknowledgments

I could not have written this book alone. Several people have helped make it possible.

I want to thank the many individuals who were willing to take the time to be interviewed. I appreciate their candor and sincerity. I have met many other recovering people whom I did not interview because time did not allow it. I regret not having their insights recorded.

Four seminary professors who assisted and supported me when writing the thesis out of which this book developed are Wendell Frerichs, Robert Albers, William Hulme, and Lance Barker. I wish to express my appreciation to them, as well as to Rev. Ronald North.

The three parishes in which I have served encompass many people who have inspired and encouraged me to grow in my understanding of chemical dependency. They are Trinity Lutheran in Dauphin, Manitoba; Trinity Lutheran in Cook, Minnesota; and Our Savior's Lutheran in Cloquet, Minnesota. I thank them for their concern over this problem that affects so many individuals and families in our communities.

I am grateful to Mona Brown–Anderson for her willingness to type all the drafts and for her helpful suggestions. She gave many hours of her time to this project. I am also grateful to Irene Getz of Augsburg Fortress for all her helpfulness and cooperation with me in this endeavor. Her work has been greatly valued.

My wife, Jeanne; my son, Ed; and my daughter, Sarah, have been very patient and understanding during this time of writing. I deeply appreciate their support.

Last, I express deep gratitude to my mother, who has been encouraging me for years to write this book. I know my father would have done the same had he still been alive.

Introduction

I walked into my first AA meeting in a room above a florist shop in Rugby, North Dakota. The smell of coffee was intermingled with cigarette smoke. The year was 1967. I was on internship during my third year of seminary training, and though I did not realize it at the moment, this was the beginning of my journey with the church and with AA.

It had started the previous Sunday. After worship a tall, lanky farmer named Cliff had come up to me and said, "Dennis, would you go to an open AA meeting with me tomorrow night?" I told him I knew nothing about AA and didn't know what an open meeting was. Cliff said that that was all the more reason I should come. He went on to say that an open meeting was an Alcoholics Anonymous meeting that anyone could attend.

Cliff picked me up the next evening. When we got upstairs above the florist shop, he began introducing me to some of the people already there. Everyone was on a first-name basis. I immediately sensed an acceptance from the men and women there, and there was obviously a feeling of acceptance among the members themselves.

I had no idea of what was going to occur in the next hour. The meeting started with a moment of silence, and I, along with everyone else, began listening to a man "tell his story." I found myself laughing along with the others as he described in vivid detail some of his insane behavior from the past. Minutes later I found myself swallowing hard, fighting back the emotions I felt welling up in me as he described the pain he had experienced. I noticed that others let the tears flow as they listened. They were free to do that. I wasn't.

That night I heard those people talk with an openness and honesty I had experienced nowhere else before. I heard more talk about God and faith and prayer than I had heard in any other place. Sure, I had heard all of these subjects in seminary and in the church, but what I heard in this room was different. Here was an open sharing of faith, struggles, defeats, victories, sorrows, and joys. They had found something; they had been given a new life they hadn't had before. An attitude of gratitude and appreciation permeated the room. I could feel their compassion, concern, and understanding.

I sat there fascinated by what I was hearing and seeing. When the group leader said it was time to close, everyone around me stood up, those on either side of me grabbed my hands, and they began praying the Lord's Prayer. I couldn't. I was too caught up emotionally by these people and by this moment. I couldn't say a word.

Cliff offered me a ride back to my home. I told him thanks but that I would walk. I will never forget that walk home. I said to myself, "This is the greatest group on earth!" I too had discovered something that night: I had discovered the fellowship of Alcoholics Anonymous. I had already experienced the fellowship of the church, but this was something different. I believed these two groups or communities had much to give to each other. I envisioned that if bridges could be built between people in AA and people in the church, each group would benefit from the other.

I was soon to find out that my new vision was not shared by everyone. In fact, it was shared by very few. In the years to follow, I found that many pastors and church members not only knew nothing about AA, but some looked upon alcoholics as the rejects of society. Alcoholics were not worth the pastor's time, it seemed, because "they wouldn't change anyway"! One pastor told me he would go to an open AA meeting only if he could preach a sermon. I don't think he ever made it.

I certainly got my ears full from those in the AA community as well. When I talked about church or worship, I often received comments like "*This* is my church!" (meaning their AA meeting) or "Those people in church wouldn't want *me* there" or "Those people who sit in the front row on Sunday morning are out cheating their neighbor on Monday."

This is not to say that I never found any AA people in church, because I did. I know people who began attending AA and church simultaneously, and they tell me that components of both AA and the Christian church enriched their recovery.

What are the ties or bridges between those in the AA community and those in the church? Where do we find them? I believe the common resource for both AA and the church is the Bible. This holy book is the authority upon which the church bases its beliefs and purpose. It is to be the source of our faith and the pattern for the way we conduct our lives. As we look at the Twelve Steps of the AA program and their origin, we soon realize that the Bible had a profound influence on the cofounders of Alcoholics Anonymous, Bill Wilson and Dr. Bob Smith.

Both men had been participants in a Christian revival or renewal movement known as the Oxford Group Movement. This Christian movement naturally based its principles upon Scripture. These biblical principles found their way into the Twelve Steps under the direction of Bill W. and, in my opinion, under the guidance of the Holy Spirit.

It is my intention now to identify these biblical bridges. Those in the church and those in AA may find common ground on these bridges upon which to develop a deeper understanding of, communication with, and appreciation for each other.

Before we examine the Twelve Steps in light of the Bible, it is essential to briefly look at the Oxford Group Movement. (Other books containing information on the Oxford Group Movement are *Not God—A History of Alcoholics Anonymous* by Ernest Kurtz and *Alcoholics Anonymous Comes of Age* by AA World Services, Inc.)

1

The History of Alcoholics Anonymous

The Oxford Group Movement

Dr. Frank Nathan Daniel Buchman, the founder of the Oxford Group Movement, was born in 1878 in Pennsburg, Pennsylvania. After graduating from Muhlenberg College, he enrolled in Philadelphia Seminary and completed his studies there in 1902.

In 1908, while attending a spiritual conference in northwestern England, Buchman became convicted of his sin and experienced a vision of Christ. He was deeply moved by this experience, and it was to have a profound influence on his later ministry.

Buchman returned to America and almost immediately was appointed secretary to the YMCA at Pennsylvania State College. Under his dynamic leadership, enrollment at the college doubled. Buchman organized spiritual conferences, taught Bible classes, and organized small voluntary Bible studies. He persuaded students to "listen to God" through Bible reading, "quiet time," and "morning watch." He repeatedly challenged his followers to live lives based upon the highest values of purity and honesty they knew.

One night in December 1921, Buchman was riding in a railroad berth to Washington, D.C. At this time he served on the faculty of Hartford Seminary, a small nonsectarian theological school in Hartford, Connecticut. His evangelistic work among the students had led to factions, not only among students, but among faculty members as well. This deeply troubled Buchman. His thoughts revolved around this controversy as he rode to Washington.

He sensed a need for greater freedom than he experienced at Hartford. Buchman's mission was to convert the world, and the means of accomplishing this would come through direction from God. Buchman spent that train ride in "quiet time" listening for God's message. When he got off the train the next morning, Buchman believed God had guided him in the evangelistic method he should use. This revelation was the inspiration for what became known as the Oxford Group Movement.

The Oxford Group Movement was to be a Christian revolution. Its goal was to begin or renew a vital Christian life for its followers. It would have no official membership. It was to be a group of people who had surrendered their lives to God and desired to live lives guided only by the Holy Spirit.

The central focus of the Oxford Group's endeavor was the "changed life." *Change* was simply the group's term for conversion. Since the words *conversion* and *evangelism* had an uncomfortable connotation for many people, this terminology was avoided. The "changed life" was viewed as the reorientation of an individual toward a better life. The primary objective in world mission was to change the individual lives of people rather than to attempt to change the political, social, or economic systems. The stages involved in the process of changing the individual were confidence, confession, conviction, conversion, and continuance.

The process of changing lives was accomplished chiefly through the practice of the "house party." These parties were held in private homes and were meant to create an informal atmosphere in which sharing, confession, fellowship, and "life-changing" were employed under the guidance of the leader. The Bible was to be studied at house parties for its importance to the individual and the group.

The Eight Points

The Oxford Group's theological emphasis revolved around what were known as the "Eight Points." Each point had a biblical basis: surrender, sharing, restitution, quiet time, guidance, witness, fellowship, and the Four Absolutes (absolute love, absolute honesty, absolute unselfishness, and absolute purity). These points were vital not only in changing lives of individuals, but also in empowering them to continue to live changed lives. Great emphasis was placed on the life of Christ, the power of the Holy Spirit, the need for daily meditation, the need for Christian fellowship, and being a witness for Christ to all people.

The Oxford Group Movement was seen by its followers as God's gift to the world to meet the needs of the 20th century. The leaders repeated frequently that God has a plan for every person on earth in addition to a divine plan for the world. As people continued to surrender themselves to God in absolute love, honesty, purity, and unselfishness, God's plan would become more known and realized by others. Christ had promised that his Spirit would guide his people into all the truth.

The Oxford Group Movement flourished during the 1900s. Although it received criticism from some of the supporters of organized religion, it had a profound effect upon thousands of individuals. The founders of Alcoholics Anonymous and those in the early history of AA were greatly influenced by their involvement in and knowledge of the Oxford Group Movement.

In order to gain a greater knowledge of the formation of AA, we will examine the stories of two men, Bill W. and Dr. Bob; their lives prior to and after sobriety; their involvement in the Oxford Group Movement; and their founding of AA and the Twelve Steps.

Bill W.

William Wilson was a successful stockbroker in New York City in the mid-1920s. He would admit later in his life that he made far too much money too quickly at his young age. During this time his drinking increased substantially.

Abruptly in October 1929, at age 33, Bill's dreams shattered with the stock market crash. Everything he had acquired in wealth melted away. His arrogance caused him to believe that he could build it all back up again. He had done it once before when he had suffered financial loss and he thought he could do it again. But this time he could not.

Early in life Bill had struggled with a feeling of inadequacy. Now that feeling overwhelmingly returned to haunt him. He began to drink more heavily. His obsession with alcohol now controlled his life. Years later Bill admitted in a speech: "I was sinking. . . . Finally, I slid down into a state where I was not drinking to dream dreams of power; I was drinking to numb the pain, to forget."[1]

During 1933–34 Bill was admitted three or four times to the Charles B. Towns Hospital, a "drying-out" facility on Central Park West. During one of these visits Bill met Dr. William Duncan Silkworth. He painted a desperate picture for Bill of allergy, obsession, and compulsion. He explained to Bill that his alcoholism was an illness; Bill had become allergic to alcohol. The doctor went on to say that even with an understanding of the physical allergy, the mind of an alcoholic was so obsessed with drinking that he drank against his own will. Silkworth warned that if Bill, or any alcoholic, ingested alcohol, even the smallest drink, he would become totally unable to control any further drinking.

Silkworth held out hope, and Bill trusted him. Bill believed he had found an answer to his problem. He would work with the doctor to overcome this obsession to drink. This new self-knowledge would help conquer his problem. Bill was sure he would never drink again.

But Bill's sobriety was short-lived. He began drinking again in three weeks. Silkworth told Bill that he was hopeless. He believed that Bill could never sober up for any length of time.

One day in November 1934 Bill was sobering up from a drinking episode when he received a phone call from his old drinking companion Ebby. Ironically, Bill had judged that Ebby was a hopeless alcoholic. Ebby asked if he could come over to see Bill. Bill was amazed when he saw his old friend later on that day. Ebby looked healthy; a new life radiated from him. Bill asked, "Come, what's all this about?" Ebby looked straight at Bill, smiled, and replied, "I've got religion."[2]

Ebby related to Bill how he had found a fellowship of people in an Oxford Group. Ebby spoke of his surrender, confession, restitution, and even his practice of prayer. He told of the release he felt from the power of alcohol; he had not had a drink for months.

Bill listened, but he did not stop drinking. However, Ebby's words haunted him, and curiosity caused him to explore what Ebby had discovered. He chose to seek out more information about the Oxford Group at its headquarters, the old Calvary Church where the Reverend Samuel Shoemaker was rector.

Attending a Calvary Church Bowery Mission service, Bill was deeply moved spiritually. He went forward for an altar call, talked with people in the mission, and talked with his wife Lois far into the night after he went home. He felt a ray of hope. He realized that he had come home without any desire or thought about going into a bar.

But the next day Bill resumed drinking. Once again he ended up in Towns Hospital in a drunken stupor. Once again Dr. Silkworth admitted him. And once again Ebby came to visit him. Ebby rephrased what he had told Bill in his home: "Realize you are licked, admit it, and get willing to turn your life over to the care of God."[3]

Ebby left the hospital room, and Bill sank into a depression that caused him to feel he was in a bottomless pit. He rebelled against the notion of a Power greater than himself. However, with his pride crushed, he cried out, "If there is a God, let Him show Himself! I am ready to do anything. Anything!"[4]

Suddenly the room lit up with a great white light. Later Bill described his experience in these words:

> I was caught up into an ecstasy which there are no words to describe. It seemed to me, in the mind's eye, that I was on a mountain and that a wind not of air but of spirit was blowing. And then it burst upon me that I was a free man. Slowly the ecstasy subsided. I lay on the bed, but now for a time I was in another world, a new world of consciousness. All about me and through me there was a wonderful feeling of Presence, and I thought to myself, "So this is the God of the preachers!" A great peace stole over me and I thought, "No matter how wrong things seem to be, they are still all right. Things are all right with God and His world."[5]

Bill explained his experience to Dr. Silkworth. The doctor referred to Bill's vision as a "conversion experience" and "psychic upheaval." He claimed that spiritual experiences could release people from alcoholism. His advice to Bill was: "Hang onto it. It is better than what you had a couple of hours ago."[6]

Ebby again visited his friend. Hearing about Bill's spiritual experience, he brought Bill *The Varieties of Religious Experience*, a book by William James. Bill read it carefully and concluded from James that although spiritual experiences were gifts that could come suddenly or gradually into people's lives, the primary significance of these experiences was that they could transform people. This new insight was to be an important factor in the history of Alcoholics Anonymous.

Along with Dr. Silkworth, Ebby had related to Bill the hopelessness of Bill's alcoholism. This was "deflation and hope" communicated from one alcoholic to another. Bill saw this essential ingredient as one part of his recovery. The other part, or "second half," was the necessity of a spiritual conversion. Both parts, Bill realized, were essential in the recovery from alcoholism.

Bill now associated himself with Oxford groups. He and Ebby worked at both Dr. Shoemaker's Calvary Mission and the Towns Hospital. However, to Bill's discouragement, the Oxford Group members were quite unenthusiastic about trying to sober up drunks. They had made the attempt in the past with little success. In fact, they became very cool toward Bill and his mission.

Dr. Bob

While staying in the Mayflower Hotel in Akron, Ohio, on a business trip, Bill was seized with the urge to get drunk. He panicked. He knew at that moment he needed another alcoholic to talk to. This was a landmark moment in Alcoholics Anonymous history! Through a telephone conversation with a Reverend Walter Tunks, Bill was given the name of Henrietta Seiberling, an Oxford Group member in Akron. Bill called her and told her the situation. Henrietta said that she was not an alcoholic, but she did know a doctor who might be beneficial for Bill to speak with. The doctor was Dr. Robert Smith, known as "Dr. Bob," who also was in the Oxford Group. He had tried to stop drinking but had been unsuccessful in his attempts.

Bill wanted to speak to Dr. Bob immediately. Henrietta called the Smith residence and spoke to Dr. Bob's wife, Anne. Anne said that Bob could not see Bill because it was Mother's Day and Bob always made a "big fuss" over her on Mother's Day. The truth was that Dr. Bob was so drunk at the moment that he was lying under the table, passed out.[7]

At five o'clock the next afternoon, May 11, 1935, Dr. Bob, Anne, Henrietta, and Bill met for the first time. This event would affect the lives of thousands of alcoholics around the world from that moment on.[8]

Dr. Bob had tried to control his drinking through the support of an Oxford group. He had not been as successful as Bill had been, but now there was a difference: they had each other for understanding and support. Both had come to realize that the purpose of life was not to "get," but rather to "give."

Dr. Bob and Bill W. did not have a specific plan or program for the recovery of alcoholics. The Twelve Steps were still years away. At this point their plan was simply to get anyone who wanted to sober up into an Oxford Group and receive direction from the Bible. Those parts of Scripture that were regarded as absolutely essential were the Sermon on the Mount, 1 Corinthians 13, and the Book of James.[9] The Twelve Steps and the Alcoholics Anonymous program were in the embryotic stage with no one realizing it.

The Twelve Steps

Bill W. returned to New York in September 1935. His interest in the Oxford Group had diminished because of many members' lack of enthusiasm over bringing alcoholics into the group. The Oxford Group had aimed at converting individuals of social prominence, and the persons whom Bill W. and Dr. Bob were recruiting were certainly not of that caliber. The issue was even more complicated when recovering alcoholics joined the group and wanted to remain anonymous because of their illness.

Tension mounted until the spring of 1937 when the Oxford Group in New York refused to admit a group of alcoholics into their fellowship. Bill W. realized a split was necessary and that it had to be permanent. Although the group of alcoholics needed their own fellowship in order for recovery to work, the Oxford Group with its emphasis on "fellowship," "the changed life," and "living a truly Christian life" had contributed to what later was to occur in the formation of AA and the Twelve Steps.

In the spring of 1938, Bill began work on the book *Alcoholics Anonymous*. Space does not allow a full account of the hurdles, frustrations, and heated discussions that took place over the next several months, but finally one night Bill W. sat at his desk and wrote the following words, which many still believe were divinely guided.

- We admitted we were powerless over alcohol, that our lives had become unmanageable.
- Came to believe that God could restore us to sanity.
- Made a decision to turn our wills and our lives over to the care of God.

- Made a searching and fearless moral inventory of ourselves.
- Admitted to God, to ourselves, and to another human being the exact nature of our wrongs.
- Were entirely ready to have God remove all these defects of character.
- Humbly on our knees asked Him to remove all these defects of character.
- Made a list of all persons we have harmed and became willing to make amends to them all.
- Made direct amends to such people wherever possible, except when to do so would injure them or others.
- Continued to take personal inventory and when we were wrong promptly admitted it.
- Sought through prayer and meditation to improve our conscious contact with God, praying only for knowledge of His will for us and the power to carry it out.
- Having had a spiritual experience as the result of these steps, we tried to carry this message to alcoholics, and to practice these principles in all our affairs.[10]

When Bill W. stopped writing, he numbered the new steps. They totaled twelve, a significant number to Bill, who thought of the twelve apostles. There were many debates and heated conversations among AA members over the religious wording. There would be slight changes, as the following chapters will indicate. In April 1939 the "Big Book" of Alcoholics Anonymous came into being. By the summer of 1939, all AA groups in Akron, New York, and Cleveland had disassociated themselves from the Oxford Group Movement. AA was now fully on its own. A movement that would expand around the world had been born.

CHAPTER

2

Step One

We admitted we were powerless over alcohol,
that our lives had become unmanageable.

The book *Alcoholics Anonymous*, commonly referred to as the "Big Book," describes alcoholism as "cunning, baffling, powerful!"[1] Anyone who has worked with the recovery of someone from alcoholism knows the truth of these words.

Powerlessness

There is no better word to describe the nature of alcoholism and the dilemma of the alcoholic than "powerlessness." Powerlessness simply means that despite the fact that chemical or alcohol usage is interfering with some persons' ability to properly manage their lives, they still cannot quit or adequately control their use of alcohol.[2] This urge to use alcohol and/or other drugs takes precedence over their families, work, and social life. They give no regard to what substance abuse will do to their physical, mental, or emotional health.

This definition of powerlessness appears simple and explicit enough, yet the inability to fully understand it, accept it, and admit it is the initial stumbling block in the efforts of many chemically dependent people to begin recovery. Society has traditionally placed the stigma of shame on anyone afflicted with alcoholism. The inability to "handle one's liquor" is seen by many as the sign of a weak person who lacks willpower.

As I stated in the preface, for my own personal research I interviewed more than 50 recovering alcoholics and counselors, all of whom I believe have some knowledge and experience with the church or the Christian faith. One of these, Dan E., came up to me on my first Sunday in my present parish. He introduced himself as a recovering alcoholic. Some months later, in a taped interview, he shared his powerlessness over alcohol and the pain it caused.

> I went to Germany in the service. There I really drank heavy. I was away from home. I was lonely. I was a martyr. So I poured down the German beer. Then I met a Christian group. I liked what they had, and I weaned off the alcohol and drugs. We traveled around together, and it was a new life for me. But about a year later I drank again. I remember that night when I got drunk. I felt so sad inside because I knew the hell had started all over again. I remember sitting outside a building crying because I was back into it again. I then went back into my old ways even stronger than ever.

No one cares to admit defeat. Our natural instincts revolt against the idea of powerlessness. We want to believe and give the impression that we are in control of our lives. Admitting powerlessness is a giant step. It is the first step. And it is not easy.

Dan N. is active in his church and has served on many church and Bible camp boards. He told me about the struggle involved in admitting his powerlessness.

Everything in my life was a result of my powerlessness over alcohol. I used to say, "Powerless over alcohol! There's no way that this bottle or this shot can be more powerful than I!" But through the years that proved to be absolutely what it is—more powerful.

Unmanageability

Is it more difficult for alcoholics to accept that their lives have become unmanageable or to accept that they are powerless? I have found on occasion that alcoholics may be ready to accept their powerlessness over alcohol but are unable to accept that their lives have become unmanageable.

Alcoholics may maintain their drinking patterns because of their desire to control the people in their environment. Through manipulation, conning, and denial, the world revolves around their wishes. However, alcoholics repeatedly find themselves in a power struggle with people and circumstances in order to maintain this control. Judy H. said this to me:

I always wanted power. I wanted everything my way. I wanted everything to circle around me. I wanted everyone to listen to me and do what I wanted them to do. This was in everything. When I was drunk, I wanted the power to say, "That person couldn't hit me!" I wanted that total power. It was important for me to say, "I can control that person."

One of the misconceptions I had in earlier years (and I was not alone in my error) was that alcoholics were "skid row bums" because alcohol had dragged them into the gutter. This is far from the truth. In fact, only 2 to 3 percent of all alcoholics fall into this category. They perhaps have held well-paying jobs, operated their own businesses, or been skilled crafts-persons at the same time their alcoholism was pro-gressing. They may be ready to admit powerlessness over alcohol, but to see life as unmanageable is be-yond their recognition. They can claim their health, spouses, families, jobs (if they still have these) as proof that they are still capable of managing their lives. They think, "So what if I get intoxicated, wreck a car now and then, or get into fights at the bar?" They may be powerless, but they still can handle their lives!

The depth to which human life can become un-manageable is expressed by Virgil M., who was em-ployed as a mechanic for a construction company. He had little to do with the Christian church at the time of the following incident.

I knew I had a deep problem. I knew that some day I would have to do something about my drinking. I tried to quit but always failed. I thought of suicide but knew I didn't have the guts to do that. I was severely depressed. The only way I could think straight was to drink, sippin' all the time. . . . Toward the end I got up in the middle of the night, often it was two or three times a night, to have a drink to sleep, to keep my nerves calm enough to get some sleep. I would wake up sweating, perspiring, having cold chills, completely torn apart inside, wondering who I'm becoming, where I'm heading, because I was lost and lost badly. The last three weeks before I went to treatment I drank continuously, day or night, on the job, off the job. I was in a stupor all the time. . . . I set myself up to get caught drinking on the job. I knew I had to get help, and through the help of God, it worked. I was found by my boss passed out in my service truck. He was very kind to me. He talked to me as no one had before. He talked with compassion and love, but he told me I had to do something about my drinking or I could no longer work for him.

Immediately after treatment, Virgil returned to church, later becoming a deacon. He still works for the same construction company and is active in AA.

Denial and Surrender

One of the most prominent symptoms of alcoholism is denial of the condition. Denial is the means for survival and control. Every day, even though they suffer from a fatal condition, alcoholics play the game of denial. It is all a part of the insidious problem that destroys health, family, financial security, spirituality, and life itself.

When I begin to listen to someone taking a fifth step (chapter 5 explains what a fifth step is), I have sometimes asked, "Do you believe you are an alcoholic?" Surprisingly, the answer sometimes is "I'm not sure" or "I don't know" or "I don't think so." Even after all the time spent in treatment or in attending AA, denial continues. Needless to say, I end the fifth-step conversation at this point and encourage the person to go back to Step One.

One recovering alcoholic told me, "An alcoholic lives in 'sincere delusion.' I just felt that I was different from all other people. I functioned best with a little alcohol in me and wished other people would understand that and leave me alone!"

When I first met Art H. he was a spiritual counselor at the Mash-ka-wisen Indian treatment center in Sawyer, Minnesota. He had previously been a pastor on an Indian reservation in northern Minnesota. He spoke to me about his denial and finding surrender.

When I was in treatment my counselor said, "Art, we who are in AA are in recovery because we live by certain spiritual principles, and who should know that more than you preachers! And yet you're the biggest con artists that ever come through treatment!" She said, "Art, I know the spiritual principles in AA can sober you up."

For the first time I took an interest. Here was hope. Before this I thought that if I crammed my head full of knowledge about alcoholism, that should do it. Now my counselor talked about honesty, and I had to admit, "Art, I don't think there is an honest bone in your body!"

Well, I believe I became honest with God for the first time in my life. I said, "God, forgive me for the mess I have become. You know how hard I have tried for thirty-five years to turn this problem around. It is only getting worse, and now I'm going to die like this. I can't stop that either, and I don't want to die like this. Please forgive me for the way I've failed you, my family, and myself. Forgive me for the mess I'm in. God, can you help? Will you help me? I need your help!" Finally, in desperation, I cried, "God, please help me!"

The next morning when I woke up I felt a freedom as a human being for the first time. That was the start of my recovery.

Art presently serves as a pastor in a remote Indian reservation between Minnesota and Ontario, accessible only by boat or plane. He is a close friend who has helped me gain some understanding of the Indians' struggles. He recently wrote a book entitled *The Grieving Indian*.

The problem alcoholics constantly face is that they are becoming aware of the truth they so strongly deny. They are aware of their drunkenness. Repeatedly I have heard recovering alcoholics say that they had known for a long time prior to surrender that they had a drinking problem. However, they would not admit it or seek help. One recovering man told me he sensed a feeling of relief when stopped by a highway patrolman. He knew then that he would receive the help he was unable to ask for. Another man told me he was once riding in a car when both he and the driver were intoxicated. The driver drove off into the ditch. When the police officer arrived and asked who was driving, the man who had been the passenger said, "I was." He knew this was the way he could receive the help he knew he needed.

Alcoholics are captives. They are in bondage. Their lives are controlled by a chemical, alcohol; it is their master, and they have no choice but to submit to its power. They are trapped by an addiction, and their condition is one of despair. Many recovering alcoholics, in "telling their story," have recounted that they contemplated suicide as an escape from the despairing condition. Unfortunately, I, along with other pastors, have conducted funerals for people who saw suicide as their only escape from the bondage of alcoholism. These are truly sad occasions.

BIBLICAL BRIDGES TO STEP ONE

The Human Condition

One biblical bridge to Step One centers around powerlessness. Being powerless over alcohol is a condition from which the alcoholic cannot escape. The Bible also speaks of a human condition, a basic estrangement, which none of us can escape. We feel a powerlessness or despair over this condition. This is reflected in the words of the psalmist: "Out of the depths I cry to you, O LORD; O Lord, hear my voice. Let your ears be attentive to my cry for mercy. If you, O LORD, kept a record of sins, O Lord, who could stand?" (Ps. 130:1-3).

Some Christian churches begin their worship service with a confessional similar to these words: "Most merciful God, We confess that we are in bondage to sin and cannot free ourselves. We have sinned against you in thought, word, and deed, by what we have done and by what we have left undone. We have not loved you with our whole heart; we have not loved our neighbors as ourselves."[3]

The Book of Genesis tells us that humans were created in the image of God but that the image has been tarnished by sin and rebellion. The problem of alcoholism, along with all other human problems, is a reflection of this fallen nature confronted by humankind. Rev. Gordon Grimm, director of training and head of pastoral care at Hazelden Treatment Center, said:

> For me the parallel here in Step One is the theme of man's basic estrangement. A lot of alcoholics would like to make their alcoholism the basis of their estrangement, and they think that's what makes them different. But it is deeper than that. There are human limits and human conditions. For me, the First Step has to do with God the Creator, and we are creatures. We are not gods. We are like gods and made in God's image, but we are not limitless. We do have limits. Powerlessness, acceptance, surrender—these concepts are important working concepts of everyday life. It is important to see them as part of the whole human condition. It is easy to blame the alcoholic in our society and make him the scapegoat in this estrangement, but we are all a part of it.

As we can see, powerlessness is not a characteristic peculiar only to alcoholism. It is an appropriate term that speaks to the human condition but is also applicable to human problems other than alcoholism. Such things as food, sex, work, relationships, certain emotions, illness, and grades in school can become obsessions. They can become too powerful for us to cope with as we are. That is one reason for the growing number of Twelve-Step groups addressing such issues.

Powerlessness produces tornness. We are limited people who fail to live up to our own expectations. There is tension within us because of our human condition. No one is a perfect person. We may choose to do right, yet somehow sin is still present. We feel powerless to do what we desire to do. This dilemma is expressed in the words of the apostle Paul: "I do not understand what I do. For what I want to do, I do not do, but what I hate I do. . . . For I have the desire to do what is good, but I cannot carry it out. For what I do is not the good I want to do; no, the evil I do not want to do—this I keep on doing" (Rom. 7:15-19).

We are both saint and sinner at the same time. Martin Luther expressed this problem with the words *simul justus et peccator* ("at one and the same time justified and sinful"). If we live in a denial that this condition persists within us, our lives are filled with tension and defeat. Not until we are honest about (surrender to God) our fallen condition (our humanness) can emotional and spiritual recovery begin.

Strength in Weakness

I stated earlier that the alcoholic survives by living in denial. The admission of powerlessness is seen as weakness. This is true not only for the alcoholic; it extends into all of human life. Our pride and ego resist any admission that we are powerless over anything. We fight to be in control and to resist showing weakness.

Here is a parallel to the Christian faith. In acceptance of our weakness (surrender), we find strength, for God's strength is manifested in our weaknesses. This is not *giving up*. This is *giving in* to the reality of powerlessness, our humanness, our imperfection. The apostle Paul wrote, "For when I am weak, then I am strong" (2 Cor. 12:10).

Many recovering persons read a daily devotional book entitled *Twenty-Four Hours a Day*. The meditation for October 7 reads:

> You must always remember that you are weak but that God is strong. God knows all about your weakness. He hears every cry for mercy, every sign of weariness, every plea for help, every sorrow over failure, every weakness felt and expressed. We only fail when we trust too much in our own strength. Do not feel bad about your weaknesses. When you are weak, that is when God is strong to help you. Trust God enough, and your weaknesses will not matter. God is always strong to save.[4]

Dying to Self

Dr. Harry Tiebout, a psychiatrist and contemporary of Bill W. and Dr. Bob, worked with alcoholics in AA. His understanding of surrender was that "the old Ego must go and a new one take its place."[5] This was a growing process. It was a goal to strive for. Tiebout wrote, "Two thousand years ago, Christ preached the necessity of losing one's life in order to find it again." (See Matthew 10:39.)

Jesus indicated also that the losing of one's life was a daily event, that is, a lifelong process. He said in Luke 9:23: "If anyone would come after me, he must deny himself and take up his cross daily and follow me." The surrender indicated by Jesus in these passages is that which Tiebout indicated must happen to "the old Ego."

Although the Bible does not refer to the ego as such, it recognizes that in the life of Christians, our sinful nature is a powerful enemy that can possess or regain control over our lives (Rom. 8:1-11).

Therefore, in the Christian faith, as well as in Step One, surrender is not a one-time event. Surrender is an attitudinal, emotional, behavioral phenomenon that needs to occur throughout life. Judy H., a recovering alcoholic, expressed it well as she spoke of her surrender:

> I don't believe I have made one complete, total surrender that takes care of everything. I grab things back again. I fall into self-pity, or I want to do things on my own. I could take a good situation and make it bad. There is fighting within myself now and then, and I have to surrender that—again. I guess that will always go on.

Grace

The grace of God is a central biblical truth. AA realizes that the new life of sobriety and sanity for the alcoholic is a gift of God's grace. Grace is a gift offered by God to us with the special purpose of accomplishing for us that which we cannot achieve for ourselves. It is the opposite of a reward for an accomplishment; it is a means of rescuing us from repeated failure and a state of helplessness.

In surrender alcoholics give in, quit fighting, admit powerlessness, and receive strength from God to do what they previously could not do themselves. God spoke to the apostle Paul, "My grace is sufficient for you, for my power is made perfect in weakness" (2 Cor. 12:9). God has accomplished in the alcoholic what previously had been impossible by human effort.

In the "Big Book" Bill W. related how the reality of grace was revealed to him when his friend Ebby came to meet him and tell him about his new discovery:

> But my friend sat before me, and he made the point-blank declaration that God had done for him what he could not do for himself. His human will had failed. Doctors had pronounced him incurable. Society was about to lock him up. Like myself, he had admitted complete defeat. Then he had, in effect, been raised from the dead, suddenly from the scrap heap to a level of life better than the best he had ever known!
>
> Had this power originated in him? Obviously, it had not. There had been no more power in him than there was in me at that minute; and this was none at all.[6]

All the willpower, promises, "cutting back," and "water wagons" that the alcoholic had previously attempted had ended in futility. Bill W. wrote:

> We could will these things with all our might, but the needed power wasn't there. Our human resources . . . failed utterly.
>
> Lack of power, that was our dilemma. We had to find a power by which we could live and it had to be a *Power greater than ourselves.*[7]

"Let go and let God," "Live and let live," "One day at a time," are not just catchy slogans one hears in AA meetings. These are expressions of the grace of God that has been experienced in the lives of its members. Heavy theological language is absent (to which some may say, "Thank goodness!"), but grace is witnessed in the lives and recovery of God's people.

One of the most memorable moments in my ministry that reflects this gift of grace was when I was giving Holy Communion to a woman in the hospital. She had struggled for years with alcoholism. Her body was now filled with cancer, and she was "skin and bones." She had asked if she could receive Holy Communion. During our bedside conversation I shared with her how by God's grace we can receive eternal life. I read Ephesians 2:8: "For it is by grace you have been saved, through faith—and this not from yourselves, it is the gift of God." When I handed her the wafer with the words, "This is the Body of Christ, given for you," she broke down and cried, "I don't deserve this!" I replied, "None of us do, Sylvia. Take and eat."

Step One starts alcoholics and other affected persons on a lifelong process of recovery. If they were to stop living the steps at this point, they would deprive themselves of the fullness of life available to them in the remaining steps. Having surrendered, recovering persons must now seek God's help if they desire to receive the quality of sobriety they realize others have. Steps Two and Three lead to hope and faith.

CHAPTER

3

Steps Two
and Three

*Came to believe that a Power greater than ourselves
could restore us to sanity.*

*Made a decision to turn our wills and lives over
to the care of God as we understood him.*

From Surrender to Faith

Out of despair comes hope. We all need hope in our
lives. Steps Two and Three bring persons into the
awareness that there is hope and that life can change.
More is needed than just the realization that their
lives are powerless over alcohol and are unmanageable. They must come to believe in a *Power greater
than themselves* if a healthy recovery is to continue.

Most often the first aspect of an addicted person's
life to be destroyed is his or her spiritual life, or
spirituality. Consequently, this is usually the last
thing to be restored. For many, a "spiritual bankruptcy" has occurred. The "Thought for the Day"
for June 9 in *Twenty-Four Hours a Day* reads:

> We finally came to the bottom. We did not have
> to be financially broke, although many of us were.

But we were spiritually bankrupt. We had a soul-sickness, a revulsion against ourselves and against our way of living. Life had become impossible for us.[1]

When a person first enters the AA program, he or she may be filled with guilt, remorse, low self-esteem, or anger. There may be little direct conversation about God at first. The Reverend Vernon E. Johnson is the founder of Johnson Institute in Minneapolis. In a personal conversation with him he said:

We certainly do not preach Christ and him crucified at first, because of the unstable emotional and spiritual condition of the person. I'd like to add the word "immediately" or "at the outset" not to do that, but that emerges as time goes on and recovery occurs.

Many surrendered alcoholics are not ready for a clearer and more definite concept of God other than "Higher Power." When one first enters the program, there may be a lot of anger and resentment toward God. As I go to different treatment centers to lecture, I can sense hostility and anger from some recently admitted clients when I tell them that I am a pastor. They may have experienced rejection from the church, from a pastor, or from "those Christian people who think they are better than everyone else." All this is interpreted by the alcoholic as judgment and condemnation by God. "If these people have nothing to do with me, then God, too, must have nothing to do with me!"

Some Christian people have difficulty with AA's use of the term "Higher Power." The term is accused of having such a vagueness that anything can be one's "Higher Power." This accusation is valid; the term "Higher Power" is open-ended. However, I appreciate what John Keller, chairman-clinical counsel, Parkside Medical Services Corporation, Park Ridge, Illinois, wrote:

> We need to recognize, first of all, that God does not necessitate faith in Jesus Christ as Lord and Savior *before* God can help a person who, in a state of surrender, is seeking help for a problem like this. Secondly, the term "Higher Power" does not limit God in helping. Most agnostic alcoholics who have difficulty even with "Higher Power" come to believe that the "Higher Power" is God if they continue to live the Twelve Steps.[2]

Certainly not every person who enters AA is an atheist or agnostic—far from that. I have listened to many people in treatment who, although they have not been in a church for years, say they never stopped believing there was a God. However, even those who claim the Christian faith (which many do) find themselves reevaluating their concept of God or "Higher Power." Gunner T. attended church all his life. He was very active, serving on church councils and boards. Though not a member of my church, I had known him for more than 25 years. He was a recovering alcoholic when he shared his experience with me:

> I think that because of my background with Christianity and because I believed I was a Christian, I had a lot of conflict with AA. When AA talked about God as a "Higher Power," it was always a single Person, some vague nothing. It certainly did not talk

about the Trinity or a personal God. I had a tough time with that. I felt guilty talking about "Higher Power" when I was a Christian. Before I took my fifth step, I vacillated between Christianity and "Higher Power" and I finally accepted God as my "Higher Power." I no longer felt guilty. After my fifth step, this became even clearer to me. My "Higher Power" was God through Christ.

Gunner T. enjoyed three years of sobriety before he died of cancer. He was a special person whom I will always remember.

AA does not dictate to recovering persons the understanding of God they are to have, as indicated in the last part of Step Three: ". . . as we understand him." It is not the intention of AA to present the concept of God in Christian terminology. However, AA must be sensitive to those persons coming into the AA program as to "where they're at" spiritually. Alcoholics need to be confronted with the reality of a Power greater than themselves. That there could be such a Power has probably never really entered their minds. They may speak about their belief in God, but subconsciously they have never really believed there existed a Power greater than themselves. When they begin to believe this, there is an opportunity for them to become more aware of God as the "Higher Power" who can supply daily help in staying sober.

Prior to this time, many practicing alcoholics have called upon God for help. They may have been raised in the Christian faith and even professed a strong faith. Like Gunner T., persons may be active in the life of a church even as their alcoholism is progressing. Alcoholics often turn to God for help in controlling their drinking or getting out of unpleasant situations. Greg R., a recovering person whom I came to know very well, said: "When I was drinking, I was always asking, 'God, get me out of this bind!' I was always bargaining, making promises. 'You do this for me and I'll do this for You!' " Greg laughed when telling of these promises, but at the time they were no laughing matter.

The alcoholic sadly discovers that this bargaining tactic does not work. The logical conclusion, therefore, is: "God doesn't care about me! I'm not good enough for God to listen to!" This compounds the guilt the alcoholic already feels. As the alcoholism progresses there is more anguish, emptiness, loneliness, and mental pain. The addicted person concludes that either there is no God at all, for God would not allow this much suffering to occur to any human being, or, if there is a God, God has certainly forsaken him or her. Bob W., a former chemical dependency counselor, said:

I felt that I must not be a good person. If I really believed in God, I could handle my problems and straighten out my life. It didn't work, but I really was not in a condition to understand anything spiritual. . . . The opinion I had formed about myself was that I wasn't worthy, and that's why these things were going on. I got to a point where I figured, "Hell, I'll just live my own life without God!" I blocked God out after that. But there was always something gnawing away, making me wonder why I felt like I did.

David H. shared:

I believed God made my dad and sister die. God had made my life miserable. . . . When I sobered up, it was a big step just to trust him, because I had hated him. I had despised God. I thought it was ridiculous that anybody could trust that.

Both Bob W. and David H. joined a church some years after becoming sober. Neither joined the church they had attended as a child.

During the progression of this addiction another god emerges which offers a pseudoreligious experience: alcohol. It is the answer to problems, religious searching, fear, inadequacy, loneliness, and emptiness. No doubt it was this realization that prompted Bill W. to write, "Before AA, we were trying to find God in a bottle."[3]

This god, alcohol (it could be food, sex, relationships, money, gambling—the list goes on and on), begins to lose its pseudoreligious power. It no longer gives meaning, relief, pleasure, and that desired "high," or euphoria, as it did before. This god betrays its followers, and they begin to recognize it as one that can ultimately destroy them.

BIBLICAL BRIDGES TO STEPS TWO AND THREE

Faith: The Work of the Holy Spirit

Bill W.'s world had collapsed. There was nowhere to turn other than to a Power greater than himself, which he had thought was nonexistent or at least beyond his reach. It was this revelation that prompted him to write in the "Big Book":

We finally saw that faith in some kind of God was part of our makeup, just as much as the feeling we

have for a friend. Sometimes we had to search fear-
lessly, but He was there. He was as much a fact as
we were. We found the Great Reality down deep
within us. . . .[4]

. . . God restored us all to our right minds. To
. . . [some] the revelation was sudden. Some of us
grew into it more slowly. But He has come to all who
have honestly sought Him.[5]

Upon initial reading, this statement may appear
to place too much emphasis on the individual's activity rather than on God's. When one takes a closer
look, however, it is clear that God is viewed as the
active one; for example, "God restored us all . . . ,"
"God has come to all. . . ." When one begins to
look for a bridge from Steps Two and Three to the
Bible, one is led to the work of the Holy Spirit in a
person's life.

Those of us who come out of a Lutheran tradition
may recall memorizing (or being asked to memo-
rize!) these words of Martin Luther: "I believe that
by my own reason and strength I cannot believe in
Jesus Christ my Lord or come to him, but the Holy
Spirit has called me through the Gospel, enlightened
me with his gifts, and sanctified and preserved me
in the true faith."[6]

I realize that Luther was referring to the Holy
Spirit calling people to faith in Christ. I realize also
that it is not the aim of Steps Two and Three to
make people believe in Jesus Christ as their Higher
Power (although that may happen). However, it
must be remembered that the steps of AA go back
to the Oxford Group, and they contain biblical principles. Although the Higher Power, or God as we
understand him, is certainly not meant to be a direct

parallel to Jesus Christ, that does not mean that there can be no parallel to Jesus Christ. The bridge has to do with coming to faith, and that is the Holy Spirit's doing.

Faith is the result of God's Spirit in our lives. Jesus said, "I have much more to say to you, more than you can now bear. But when he, the Spirit of truth, comes, he will guide you into all truth" (John 16:12-13).

Certainly the Holy Spirit has not excluded alcoholics from growing in faith and knowledge of Jesus. Alcoholics in their spiritual bankruptcy have much to learn about God (as we all do), much more than they can comprehend at first. They must, therefore, begin with the thought or belief in a Power greater than themselves. Many alcoholics and other recovering persons, in looking back upon their "coming to believe," realize it was not their doing, but it "happened." It was a gift given out of the grace of a Power whom they are coming to understand as God. They may begin to see themselves on the threshold of a journey of faith. This faith in the God of their understanding is taking them into an unknown future one day at a time.

In 1 Corinthians 13:9-12, the apostle Paul gives us a glimpse of how he sees his journey of faith: "For we know in part and we prophesy in part, but when perfection comes, the imperfect disappears. When I was a child, I talked like a child, I thought like a child, I reasoned like a child. When I became a man, I put childish ways behind me. Now we see but a poor reflection as in a mirror; then we shall see face to face. Now I know in part; then I shall know fully, even as I am fully known."

Steps Two and Three entrust addicted persons to the grace of God. In neither step is there pressure that "you must believe this" or "you must accept that." Beginning with a "Power greater than ourselves," recovering persons are to let God freely reveal himself in the Spirit's own way and time. "Let go and let God" is a slogan that points to the fact that one's spirituality cannot be rushed. "Seek and you will find," said Jesus. By living in God's grace, people place themselves in God's timetable and open themselves to the direction of God's Spirit.

David H., a recovering person, chemical dependency counselor, and converted Christian, believes that the Holy Spirit used the steps of AA to bring him into an awareness of Jesus Christ. He tells of his spiritual journey:

> God led me to know Jesus through the AA program. I guess it's like coming in the back door, but it worked.
>
> I remember getting down on my knees in treatment and saying, "I can't do it! My life is yours!" I surrendered to God as I knew Him, and it was not Jesus at that time. I was not a Christian for another two years.
>
> I kept in the spiritual part of the program. I kept searching. I read the Bible. I talked with people. . . . Through AA, going to meetings, going over the steps, God kept me going in the right direction. I even visited different churches. I know the Holy Spirit was leading me. My mom had prayed for me throughout all my drinking years, and now I know her prayers were answered.
>
> I then met a girl whom I had previously taken to detox. She had a certain look about her now. She was different. She invited me to her church, and I

went there. I saw a lot of love between people. Eventually I got saved and gave my life to Christ.

Now Christ is real to me. AA is a program, but I believe the Lord works through it. I believe that if you turn your life and will over to God, God's gift is his Son, Jesus. . . . you will find Christ. Or, I should really say, Christ will find you.

The terminology of "being saved" may not be common language to everyone. However, whether familiar or comfortable, the point is clear that the work of the Holy Spirit is an appropriate topic for conversation and as a bridge between those in the church and those in AA and other Twelve-Step groups. Let us look at another bridge closely related to this one, "conversion."

Conversion: A Spiritual Transformation

Conversion may or may not be a frequently used word in your spiritual vocabulary. Nevertheless, it is a biblical concept, and it certainly ties into Steps Two and Three.

Conversion, in the biblical sense, means a "turning" or "returning." The verb forms of *conversion* are found in both the Old and New Testaments. In the Old Testament, turning to God, or conversion, is more than a change of mind or undergoing some experience. It is a concrete change to a new way of life, as the word *turn* suggests. It is, however, always viewed as an act of an individual made possible only by the previous act of God.

In the New Testament, this "turning" is often associated with repenting, as in Acts 3:19 and 26:20. It is also associated with believing, as in Acts 11:21.

The biblical emphasis is upon an objective change in a person. The change is not achieved by some outward act as Pharisees and others practiced, but rather a true turning to God through repentance and belief leads not only to an observable new way of life, but to a spiritual transformation or change as well. Paul writes in 2 Corinthians 3:18, "And we, who with unveiled faces all reflect the Lord's glory, are being transformed into his likeness with ever-increasing glory, which comes from the Lord, who is the Spirit." Conversion is totally the work of the Holy Spirit in the intellect, will, and emotions of a human being.

Although the Oxford Group attempted to avoid the word *conversion* in their meetings, the idea of a "changed life" certainly prevailed in conversation and literature. Those in the group taught that God had a plan for each person's life. The means of discovering one's life plan was the absolute surrender of one's life to God. All of life must be turned over to God. The challenge the Oxford Group presented to its members was: Are you willing to let God run your life, or will you keep it in your own hands? This teaching and challenge was influential and inspirational in the formulation and purpose of Steps Two and Three.

The conversion in AA is the turning from drinking to not drinking. It is a turning from the condition of active alcoholism to a total life-style called "sobriety." It is a conversion from a destructive, self-centered life to one that is constructive, creative, and positively interactive with others.

The theme of spiritual change (conversion) through the grace of God emerges repeatedly throughout the literature of AA. Bill W. wrote in the "Big Book":

> The great fact is just this, and nothing less: that we have had deep and effective spiritual experiences which have revolutionized our whole attitude toward life, toward our fellows, and toward God's universe. The central fact of our lives today is the absolute certainty that our Creator has entered into our hearts and lives in a way which is indeed miraculous. He has commenced to accomplish those things for us which we could never do by ourselves.[7]

The conversion, or transformation, of life is not a goal toward which a person strives; rather it is the acceptance of a gift that is given. Wishing, willing, working, and worrying accomplish nothing. This change is the result of God's power. Again, Bill W. wrote, ". . . our human resources, as marshalled by the will, were not sufficient; they failed utterly. Lack of power, that was our dilemma. We had to find a power by which we could live, and it had to be a power greater than ourselves."[8]

Bill W. himself experienced a "spiritual awakening" shortly after being hospitalized for his last "drunk" (see chapter 1). The day after this experience, Bill W. was introduced to the book *Varieties of Religious Experiences* by William James. Bill W. made this conclusion:

> Spiritual experiences, James thought, could have objective reality; almost like gifts from the blue, they could transform people. Some were sudden brilliant illuminations; others came on very gradually. Some flowed out of religious channels; others did not. But nearly all had the common denominators of pain,

suffering, calamity. Complete hopelessness and deflation at depth were almost always required to make the recipient ready.[9]

Although the word *conversion* is seldom used by recovering alcoholics, the phenomenon described by many in their "spiritual experience," or awakening, is certainly a parallel with the biblical turning to God with a spiritual transformation following.

Virgil M. described the spiritual renewal, or conversion, that he experienced in the first days of his recovery:

Early in treatment my counselor asked me how I felt about my God, and I told her I believed. I thought God had kind of let me down at times, but I know now who let whom down.

Anyway, she said, "When you go home tonight I suggest that both you and your wife get down on your knees and turn your life over to your God."

I think this moment was the most heartwarming and one of the biggest events of my sobriety, because when we got home that night, we got down on our knees. . . . I can't really remember all I said or in what order, but I know I asked him to forgive my past and to take the craving, the desire for alcohol, away then and forever. And to this day, I don't have one. I haven't had a desire or "a want" to drink again. It's been completely taken away to this day.

In a private conversation, David B. told me of his conversion experience, which had occurred two years before while he was in treatment.

I was sitting on the edge of my bed. I felt terrible. I felt everything was hopeless. If I could have ended my life at that moment, I would have. Out of despair

I cried out: "God, you have to help me! Take my life!" Suddenly I felt a power or force seize me. I began to tremble. I could not stop myself. I cried out again: "Oh, God, help me!" The trembling stopped, and I felt a Presence come over me. It was like water poured over me. It went throughout my whole body. I felt a great peace; a great joy was welling up in me. I was free! I knew it! I knew that this was God's doing! I realize now that I was touched by the power of the Holy Spirit.

David B. then became active in both AA and a church. He had attended neither one before. Two weeks after our conversation I was deeply saddened to hear that David was killed in a car-train accident. He had two years of sobriety. His spiritual experience was a moving one for me to listen to. May it now live on.

Both Virgil M. and David B. described vividly a conversion or transformation experience. Transforming experiences could be told by countless other recovering people. This empowering event from God became a turning point in their recovery to a new life. In their experience there was self-surrender. They "gave up" trying; they "let go and let God," as the AA slogan suggests. Their experience was an objective one in the sense that it was not something they generated from within themselves. It was the action of a Power outside their own being.

The apostle Paul invites his readers to allow this power of God to transform them inwardly: "So then, my brothers, because of God's many mercies to us, I make this appeal to you: Offer yourselves as a living sacrifice to God, dedicated to his service and pleasing to him. This is the true worship that you should offer. Do not conform outwardly to the standards of this world, but let God transform you inwardly by a complete change of your mind. Then you will be able to know the will of God. . ." (Rom. 12:1-2 TEV).

Hope: Confidence for the Future

Hope is a great biblical word that has a rich meaning for all of us but especially for alcoholics. Often when I lecture at a treatment center I say, "You don't have to raise your hand, but how many of you came to a point where life for you felt hopeless?" Invariably, hands will go up. These people have experienced a hell on earth. I don't know what hell is like, but certainly the atmosphere and outlook must be hopeless.

Powerlessness has now been admitted. These people are beginning to believe that maybe, just maybe, there is a Power that can help them to stay sober so that they can make some sense out of their lives. Hope is coming back. They begin to feel some confidence for the future. It is not an overwhelming feeling that suddenly engulfs them; rather it is a tiny light that has begun to burn in their dark, hellish world, a world that has existed for many months or years.

Hope may die for alcoholics, but it needs to live in the hearts of their families and friends. This I learned early in my ministry. During my internship I discovered that one of the people in my new-member class was a practicing alcoholic. When his drinking got him into one problem after another, Cliff, who took me to that first open meeting, asked what I thought would happen to this man. I replied that I thought he was hopeless. Cliff said, "No, Dennis, he's not hopeless. As long as there's life, there's hope!" I have never forgotten his words. I have been privileged to see their truth.

The hope found in Steps Two and Three certainly bridges over to the hope the disciple Peter wrote about in his first letter: "Let us give thanks to the God and Father of our Lord Jesus Christ! Because of his great mercy, he gave us new life by raising Jesus Christ from the dead. This fills us with a living hope, and so we look forward to possess the rich blessings that God keeps for his people" (1 Pet. 1:3-4 TEV). Recovering alcoholics have gone through a death and resurrection experience at this point on the road to recovery, and a living hope has begun to spring up within them.

As this chapter comes to a close, we see that the overarching bridge from the Bible into Steps Two and Three is the activity of the Holy Spirit. God's Spirit guides people to faith, turns their lives in conversion, and supplies hope to them as they discover a new life. Over this bridge, deeper communication, appreciation, and understanding can pass between all of us.

CHAPTER

4

Step Four

Made a searching and fearless moral inventory
of ourselves.

A Look at Self

The Oxford Group encouraged personal inventory
and referred to it as a "daily checking." Group members evaluated their lives against Four Absolutes:
love, honesty, unselfishness, and purity. These absolutes were to be a guide to the surrendered person.
They were indicators revealing where additional surrender was needed.

Although Step Four calls for recovering persons
to take inventory of their entire lives, it is my contention that the "daily checking" of the Oxford
Group was influential in the need for Step Four (and
also Step Ten). Bill W. came to know the importance
of personal inventory.

Steps Four and Five are often met with the most
resistance for those following the Twelve-Step program. It is a threatening experience for most of us
to take a searching and fearless moral inventory of
ourselves. There is wisdom in the words "searching"
and "fearless." No one is benefited by seeing and
criticizing the faults and weaknesses of other people.

Jesus realized that it was always easier for us to examine and point out the speck in our neighbor's eye than to notice the log in our own eye (Matt. 7:3-5). The fourth step examines the logs.

Obviously there are some things in alcoholics' lives that need changing. (This is true for all of us.) Now that they have sobered up, they need to look honestly at their lives with a clear head. It does take fearlessness to take a look at "me," but it is advantageous to recovering persons if they can uncover some of their personality characteristics from which alcohol initially provided an escape. Therefore the inventory involved in Step Four is not just a matter of alcoholics looking at their drinking behavior. It is a time to look honestly at their selfishness, dishonest thinking, pride, resentments, fear, impatience, jealousy, procrastination, and self-pity. Certainly these are common to all humans, but for alcoholics they are tied to uncontrollable drinking. Alcohol had been a great escape from looking at their innermost feelings. We read in the book *Twelve Steps and Twelve Traditions*, known as "12 X 12":

> We had drunk to drown feelings of fear, frustration, and depression. We had drunk to escape the guilt of passions, and then we have drunk again to make more passions possible. We have drunk for vain glory—that we might the more enjoy foolish dreams of pomp and power. This perverse soul sickness is not pleasant to look upon. Instincts on the rampage balk at investigation. The minute we make a serious attempt to probe them, we are liable to suffer severe reactions.[1]

Exposure to our self and our behavior is a fearful experience. However, it is essential to expose our life and actions to reveal some of the fundamental problems that led many of us into the condition of alcoholism and other addictions. The "Big Book" refers to resentment as the "number one" problem or attitude that can enslave and destroy a person.[2]

Occasionally I listen to people who do not want to "let go" of their resentment. I recall a man who said repeatedly, "I'll never forgive them. I'll hate them until I die!" I asked if he really wanted to continue to live in such deep resentment. His answer was, "Yes!" He had been in treatment over a dozen times. His resentment and the intense anger provided him an excellent excuse to drink again whenever the urge came.

Unresolved resentment can reveal itself in a variety of ways in the alcoholic's life. However, in addition, such emotions as jealousy, false pride, guilt, anger, hurt, shame, and a sense of inferiority have played a dramatic role in the alcoholic's behavior. His or her life has been one of covering up, pretending, escaping, running, and denying. The fourth step is a day of reckoning.

Throughout this step the person is doing more than just looking at "something about myself." He or she is realizing, "This is me!" Healing and growth begin to occur only when these destructive emotions are faced honestly. The fourth step is a step of freedom as it begins to move alcoholics away from the emotions of guilt, shame, resentment, and many others that have enslaved them in the past.

Step Four may hold a profound revelation. Just because alcoholics are now sober does not mean that their problems and destructive feelings have automatically disappeared. I need to clarify my use of "destructive feelings." Most of us struggle with feelings of resentment, anger, guilt, and jealousy. These are all normal human feelings. They become destructive when they are verbally unexpressed, denied, or covered up. The inventory of Step Four reveals that these feelings are still present even though the alcoholic has not been drinking. For instance, a man may still resent the way his boss treats him. He still argues with his wife. His problems have not only failed to disappear now that he is sober, they seem to have grown worse! He is now aware of the feelings that never bothered him when he was drunk. Previously he did not have to deal with them. Alcohol anesthetized them. It provided the escape. Now he has to face them in Step Four and even write about them!

Recovering persons may discover that their troubles belong to the department of "causes" instead of "effects." This is not to say that these troubles or feelings were the cause of someone becoming an alcoholic. What causes a person to become an alcoholic is still unproven. I believe, however, that these emotions, previously denied and stuffed away, contributed to the progression of the disease.

For example, it was not alcohol that filled people's lives with fear; it was fear that contributed to their alcoholism. It was not alcohol that made them feel inferior; it was a feeling of inferiority that aided the progression of their alcoholism.

Previously a woman may have used her feelings as an excuse to drink. Now, during this self-examination, she begins to realize that these are not the consequences of her alcoholism. Instead, they played a primary role in the progression of her alcoholism. Alcohol had altered her moods. It had helped her "cope" with things, or so she thought. As she takes this fourth step, she realizes that these feelings are still present and are causing her problems in living sober! Step Four can be a "sobering" experience because the excuses can no longer be used.

No one begins to drink with the intention of becoming an alcoholic. Somewhere he or she crossed that invisible line and was no longer able to say no to alcohol. From there the condition progressed to what may now be chronic alcoholism. Step Four offers recovering persons an opportunity to honestly examine the reasons and emotions around them and within them from which alcohol provided an escape.

Low Self-Image

It has been my experience, from listening to many recovering alcoholics tell their story in a fifth step, that most alcoholics struggle with feelings of shame and low self-worth. Shame says: "I am an unworthy person. I am unworthy of love. I am of no value. I am a bad person." Years of drinking can severely damage an alcoholic's self-worth, but often the feeling of shame enters long before the person begins drinking. Parents, siblings, or peers who blamed, belittled, criticized, or abused this individual made him feel ashamed. Unless this person feels acceptance coming through words and actions, he will live the rest of his life feeling, "I can never measure up! I am not good enough!"

Remember the words of the prodigal son in Luke 15: "I am not worthy to be called your son!" The depth of shame states: "I am not even worthy of *being!*" Often these feelings are concealed by false pride and arrogance. However, the feelings of un-acceptableness and self-hatred, all linked to shame and guilt, rage within the person. He believes that if anyone really knew what he was like or knew all he had done, no one would accept him.

Pat O. was about a year into recovery when she shared with me the depth of unacceptableness she felt toward herself:

> I didn't think there was a term to describe how low I felt. . . . I didn't think I deserved anything. I didn't think I deserved to be cared about by anyone. Anytime I would start to get involved with a man who treated me nice, I would do something to destroy that relationship because I could not handle anyone who was nice to me . . . I didn't think I deserved it or I was worth it. I had a hard time living with myself. I remember times when I would lie in bed at night and think about some of the things I had done and I could feel my face flush with shame. It was the only time I would allow myself even to cry . . . even that was after a few drinks because I wasn't worth crying over.

Loss of Spirituality

This feeling of low self-worth extends into how alcoholics view their relationship with God. Their behavior and feelings of guilt affect their spiritual life. They believe that God certainly could not tolerate their morally wrong behavior, much less accept it. God, they think, could never forgive them. Rev. Vernon Johnson said, "The alcoholic believes that God, if there be a God, would have nothing to do with the likes of me."

Alcoholics hate themselves for their actions. This self-hatred perpetuates itself. Johnson says, "It is the nature of the illness. The alcoholic has this tremendous self-hatred, and any symbol of hope, health, or righteousness that he sees in someone else intensifies this self-hatred within him." This self-hatred certainly affects alcoholics spiritually. How they view themselves projects into their conception of how God sees them. Judy H. related: "I was never turned away by the church. . . . I pushed the church and God away from me because of the hatred I had toward myself."

Many recovering persons to whom I have listened do not believe that God is capable of forgiving or accepting them. One man told me that because of what he had done, he believed his soul was in jeopardy and nothing would ever change that.

Judy H. has been sober for three years but still grapples with her feelings about herself:

> I keep trying to discipline myself in the steps. I believe I have learned how to pray. This helps me. I believe I am forgiven and have self-worth. I am a worthful person. This is all wrapped up in my belief in God. . . . Eventually I forgave myself for the things I did. But once in a while I grab some of that stuff back. I dwell on it and feel worthless again. Then I moan, "Oh, why did I do that?"

There is much truth in the statement that the spirituality of an alcoholic is the first quality to be destroyed and the last quality to return.

BIBLICAL BRIDGES TO STEP FOUR

Combating Sin

The word *sin* may cause alarm in some readers as AA does not use the term. However, when we speak of the destructive emotions, such as resentment, anger, fear, guilt, shame, false pride, inferiority, and jealousy, we recognize that these are consequences of the sinful condition present in all human beings. This means that sin is by no means the peculiar property of alcoholics. These feelings find their roots in a human's imperfection. Alcoholics have let alcohol destroy them, but this is one form of many by which people can destroy themselves. Suicide has claimed the lives of many who have never touched a drop of alcohol. There are many avenues of "escape" from facing oneself. Perfectionism, sex, work, food, sleep, blaming others, and frequently moving to new locations are all methods people may use to avoid honestly facing themselves and their inner feelings.

Step Four confronts the roots of a problem on the basis of one's behavior. It causes men and women to take ownership of their behavior and emotions. It is a painful step, but pain is often necessary for the restoration of health.

There is an expression in some Christian circles known as "the second use of the law." This "second use" is to lead individuals to a knowledge of their sin. The law, or Ten Commandments, acts as a mirror by which people see that their actions and lives are so impure and imperfect that, by themselves, they cannot stand before God. They are in need of a savior who can remove these imperfections and impurities. Without an honest examination of one's total life, such a need for a savior is not realized. Rev. Vernon Johnson shared these words about the fourth step:

> This then is a continuation of the conversion experience in that it is a real search of self against a

moral background. I describe this as a resolution of a massive characterological conflict where behavior is recognized now as being in direct conflict to what is now again a recognized value system. The emotion through which this happens is the emotion called guilt. . . . It is a recognition of a value system which was believed to have disappeared. "I used to be, but I'm not. . . ." If I feel this guilt, then the value is still present. If I feel guilty about something, then I'm committed to a value that says, "I'm wrong!"

The parallel [or bridge] to the Christian position is that it is through our guilt and shame we come to know God's grace in Christ and his cross.

AA brings people into a continuous program of freedom from the human condition (sin) in their lives that would make them active alcoholics again except for the sustaining Higher Power operating to overcome the defects of character brought out in this personal inventory.

Christianity does the same. God seeks to redeem men and women from their sinful condition by the freeing power of the gospel (Rom. 3:23-24). In order for people to realize the Good News, their sinful condition must be recognized. Self-examination and inner searching need to be done in a Christian's life. "Let us examine our ways and test them, and let us return to the LORD" (Lam. 3:40). Jesus said, "When [the Counselor] comes, he will convict the world of guilt in regard to sin and righteousness and judgment" (John 16:8). The "second use of the law" and the fourth step provide an opportunity for the Spirit to convince people of their need for a savior. The Law (the Ten Commandments), as well as the fourth step, has the power to destroy excuses and convict a person. Romans 3:19-20 reflects this: "Now we know that whatever the law says, it says to those who are under the law, so that every mouth may be silenced and the whole world held accountable to God. Therefore no one will be declared righteous in his sight by observing the law; rather, through the law we become conscious of sin."

A New Sense of Worth

It should be noted at this point that the inventory taken by recovering persons does not have to reflect only the negative aspects of their lives. It should include positive events, characteristics, and qualities as well. There are two reasons for this.

First, it affirms to them that they are of value. Reflecting upon the positive aspects of their lives causes them to realize that they are not "all bad" as they previously felt. Through this positive reflection they begin to sense their worth in relation to themselves, others, and ultimately to God. "What is man that thou art mindful of him, and the son of man that thou dost care for him? Yet thou hast made him little less than God, and dost crown him with glory and honor" (Ps. 8:4-5 RSV).

Second, as recovering persons realize more worth in themselves, they begin to observe and respect the worth and positive qualities seen in others. They begin to view the events that touch their lives as opportunities given by God to help them grow.

Self-examination, the need for a savior, and God-given self-worth, are bridges we all need to walk on in our journey of spirituality.

5

Step Five

*Admitted to God, to ourselves, and to another
human being the exact nature of our wrongs.*

Call for Complete Honesty

This is a difficult and frightening step to take. Over
the years as I have listened to fifth steps, I have yet
to meet someone who comes to do an honest and
thorough fifth step who is not nervous and apprehensive. What makes this step so intimidating is that
it calls for complete honesty.

Let me explain the phrase "taking a fifth step."
A fifth step is a confessional, or a "tell-it-all" moment
for the recovering person. It is usually done with a
clergyperson who functions more in a listener role
than as a counselor. This step may take place at the
treatment facility or in a pastor's office. It is a time
when the recovering person shares not only specific
events that have occurred in his or her life but also
the emotions felt at the time. This step is not to be
done only once in a lifetime; rather persons are encouraged to do a fifth step on a regular basis, such
as annually or when they feel they need to do it.

The step reads, "Admitted . . . the exact nature
of our wrongs." This means that I expose myself

totally to you. It is like standing naked before someone else. Even Adam, when he discovered he was naked, ran into the bushes and tried to cover himself with fig leaves. Step Five says, "I stand before you with no fig leaves!" What frightens me is that if I am completely honest with you about all areas of my life, actions, feelings, and thoughts, you may reject me. Most of us have felt enough rejection in our lives. This is certainly true for the alcoholic. However, for those who do not yield to this fear, Step Five is a time of "letting go."

Step Five, like Step Four, is a step of freedom. Here people can take all the "rocks" (burdens, fears, guilts) that they have carried for years and "dump them." This is a liberating experience. More than once I have heard people say that they actually felt lighter as they left the room. It is as though they have experienced a rebirth. They have just told their life story in which all the closet doors have been opened and all the secrets are out. They have told all the dark areas of their life and still are accepted! For many, Step Five is a pivotal point in recovery. It is a time of "leaving behind" the past and moving forward into the future, one day at a time. The "Big Book" says it well: "We must be entirely honest with someone if we expect to live long and happily in this world."[1]

BIBLICAL BRIDGES TO STEP FIVE

Confession

It would seem obvious that the bridge from Step Five would be confession. This word, however, is avoided in the AA program because of the religious connotation some may attach to it. For many in AA, previous encounters with religion were negative ones. Therefore the writers of the Twelve Steps and the "Big Book" used the words "admitted" and "admission." The "12 X 12" reads:

> This practice of admitting one's defects to another person is, of course, very ancient. . . . [2]
>
> Most of us would declare that without a fearless admission of our defects to another human being we could not stay sober.[3]

However, biblically speaking, Step Five is a step of confession. The confession of Step Five may be viewed as a sharing of one's specific defects without the intent or expectation that an absolution or "absolving of sins" will follow. That does not mean, however, that an absolution can have no place in a fifth step. I have had the experience of a person asking for a prayer for forgiveness following his or her "admission." On other occasions I have had the person ask me, "Do you think God has forgiven me?"

Carol R., a recovering person and a woman active in her Roman Catholic church, shared her thoughts. "For me, taking a fifth step is the same as going to confession. . . . There you admit to God and to a priest or minister the exact nature of your sins."

As you may recall from chapter 1, confession was an important aspect of the Oxford Group. The biblical passage upon which the Oxford Group based this practice was James 5:16: "Therefore confess your sins to each other and pray for each other so that you may be healed." Confession was seen as an essential ingredient for spiritual development.

In the Bible the confession of sins is an acknowledgment of one's fallenness and helplessness. The Old Testament often presents people pondering the desperation of their plight and their helplessness to escape. Confession is seen as necessary for a reconciliation with God. In confession, the individual realized the sovereignty of God and God's right over against a human being. "For I know my transgressions, and my sin is always before me. Against you, you only, have I sinned, and done what is evil in your sight, so that you are proved right when you speak and justified when you judge" (Ps. 51:3-4).

In the New Testament Jesus stressed the need for confession. The parables of the prodigal son (Luke 15:11-32; see v.18) and of the Pharisee and the tax collector (Luke 18:10-14) make confession a central ingredient in forgiveness.

Augustine said that confession is good for the soul. Confession is therapeutic. As a person confesses his or her sins to another human being, the intangibleness of God takes on a personal nature as the person experiences the listener's acceptance.

There is a risk involved in telling the exact nature of one's wrong, but it is in this telling that trust in another human being begins. The confessor may also sense a feeling of self-worth that previously had been absent. Even though AA members have shared with their AA group some of their behavior, this does not bring the same sense of acceptance Step Five can make through confession.

We read in the "12 X 12":

> When we reached AA, and for the first time in our lives stood among people who seemed to understand, the sense of belonging was tremendously

exciting . . . but we soon discovered that while we weren't alone anymore in a social sense, we still suffered many of the old pangs of anxious apartness. Until we had talked with complete candor of our conflicts . . . we still didn't belong. Step Five was the answer. It was the beginning of true kinship with man and God.[4]

David H. related to me how Step Five opened for him a new awareness of himself. It was the start of restoring his self-worth. He said:

I had never told anyone what I was like, and I found out in the fifth step that I could do that. . . . I thought before I would shrivel up and waste away if anyone were ever to find out what I really had done and what was really inside of me. It was a tremendous feeling just to find out that I could tell someone everything I had ever done. Step Five for me was a turning point. I was able to tell someone everything and leave it behind.

Freedom through Forgiveness

Another biblical bridge that emerges from Step Five is forgiveness. A new freedom found in forgiveness is the desired result of confession. It is a freeing experience that affects a person's total being. Burdens are lifted and inner torment is vanquished by God's forgiveness and pardon. Psalm 32:1-5 beautifully reflects this experience: "Happy are those whose sins are forgiven, whose wrongs are pardoned. Happy is the man whom the Lord does not accuse of doing wrong and who is free from all deceit. When I did not confess my sins, I was worn out from crying all day long. Day and night you punished me, Lord; my strength was completely drained, as moisture is dried up by the summer heat. Then I confessed my sins to you, I did not conceal my wrongdoings. I decided to confess them to you, And you forgave all my sins" (TEV).

Prior to the taking of Step Five, alcoholics carry the burdens of guilt, shame, resentment, jealousy, inferiority, and a host of other destructive, repressed emotions. They now verbalize specific failures and shortcomings recalled from memory. As a certain incident is told, the emotion that went with it is regenerated within the teller. Thus Step Five can be a very emotional time. Alcoholics have often come to believe that they are on the lowest rung of humanity. In the midst of their addiction they begin to think that there is no God. If there is such a being as God, this God would never allow humans to feel as miserable and lonely as they do. If by some remote chance there is some divine being present, it would be impossible for this God to forgive them or even accept them. They feel that they have exceeded the limits of forgiveness and acceptance from anyone, whether human or divine.

Yet it is in telling another human being the painful remembrances of the past that the awareness of forgiveness and acceptance begins to sprout and grow. If there is acceptance from the person listening to the fifth step, perhaps there also can be forgiveness and acceptance from God.

A sudden sense of freedom from guilt and shame through forgiveness and acceptance may occur during the fifth step. In other cases, a gradual awareness of forgiveness and acceptance begins and continues as the recovering person moves on in the steps. This again is the Holy Spirit's activity in the life of the person.

The Bible describes forgiveness as God graciously taking away the obstacles or barriers that separate a person from him. God opens a way to a new relationship with him.

The effect of forgiveness in the New Testament is threefold. It brings a wholeness of life, it offers freedom from guilt, and it removes any barriers between a person and God.

Wholeness of Life

The fifth step is a major step for recovering persons. It is a step away from feeling isolated and lonely; it is a step toward wholeness, inner peace, and a new sense of "accepting who I am." Martin Luther said that where there is forgiveness of sins, there is life and salvation. I prefer to describe salvation as "wholeness of life," which can begin now in this present life and will certainly continue in the life to come.

I have witnessed this "wholeness of life" begin to sprout in individuals during their fifth step. They begin their fifth step tense, nervous, fearful, often showing feelings of resentment toward me that I as a clergyperson must listen to them. As they share the painful and shame-filled memories and emotions of past events, they become more relaxed, receptive, and accepting. In their confession of the exact nature of their wrongs, a liberating and healing process begins within their lives. No longer do they attempt to justify their actions by blaming others or finding excuses. They realize they are who they are and depend solely on the grace of God for acceptance and forgiveness. Through the attention, concern, and acceptance of the listener, the Holy Spirit begins to lead recovering persons into the awareness that by God's grace forgiveness is available to them. They actually begin to sense that they are forgiven, and they know that they have done nothing to deserve this forgiveness. They are receiving it as a gift from God. Their fragmented lives are becoming whole.

Release from Guilt

The second aspect of forgiveness in the New Testament is release from guilt. Guilt is a tremendous burden carried by the alcoholic. Gunner T. said:

> In the confused state of alcoholism I could not get rid of the guilt. Every time I went to church, which was almost every Sunday, I felt guilt, remorse, and resentment. It wasn't necessarily the sermon that made me feel that. It was the fact that I was there and I was not right with God. I knew it in my heart, and I had enough guilt without the condemnation I felt. I've always been active in the church, but as the alcoholism progressed I could see myself becoming phony. It was downright hypocrisy which compounded the guilt.

The Swiss psychologist Carl Jung said that telling one's story is the very beginning of healing therapy. By doing this, a person will be relieved of the terrible burden of guilt. Many people who have completed a fifth step describe their experience as relief from a heavy weight upon them or a sense of being cleansed.

Often, in order for recovering persons to attain the peace and freedom they have searched for, a new understanding of God must occur. Many recovering people tell of growing up believing that God is a God of judgment, wrath, and punishment. Art H., a recovering alcoholic and pastor, said this about his past concept of God:

> God, for me, had always been a God who stood in judgment over me. I believed he was always waiting for me to mess up. Every time I did, he would somehow get even with me. I did not know a God of love, forgiveness, and grace.

Through the telling of one's story and unburdening of soul, a person is often appreciative that "this is *my* story." When people relive painful experiences in this step, they discover a God who is not far removed from them. Rather they discover a God who is in the midst of their suffering, protecting them and leading them to this stage of recovery. Believing in a God who offers love, forgiveness, and acceptance is a new revelation for the alcoholic and his struggle with guilt and shame. Gunner T. shared his feeling of guilt in church and went on to tell of his release in his fifth step:

> In the fifth step I dumped the guilt. . . . I was no longer under the condemnation I had always felt in church. . . . the fifth step was important to me because, after I had taken it, my Christianity became a lot more important to me. It was then that I could talk to God and feel there was forgiveness.

Some people grow up in the Christian faith but fall away as their alcoholism progresses. Greg R. was such a person. He saw his fifth step from a Christian perspective. After treatment he went back to the church and became active again.

> For me the fifth step was important. For me it had to do with forgiveness. If Christ had not died on the cross for me, I wouldn't be able to ask for forgiveness and know I had received it. After my fifth step I knew I was forgiven.

The third aspect of forgiveness in the New Testament involves the removing of barriers both between oneself and others and between oneself and God. This will be addressed specifically in Steps Eight and Nine in chapter 6.

Justification: Being Made Right with God

Justification, a "major league" word in the Bible, means being made right with God or being justified by God by grace through faith. Another way of expressing this event is God declaring a person innocent, or "not guilty." The New Testament is very clear about saying that we cannot make ourselves right with God by our own efforts. We read this in Galatians 2:15-16: "We . . . know that a man is not justified by observing the law, but by faith in Jesus Christ." We can see this same thought in Galatians 3:11 and Romans 3:28.

This gift, accomplished by God and given by God, is received by a person through believing it, that is, trusting or having faith that it is true. Faith is not simply some intellectual assent or an activity or a person's mind or emotions. Faith is a dynamic activity that involves submitting one's whole being to God. It is relying on God physically, mentally, and emotionally. Back in Step Two it was stated that faith is the result of God's Spirit being active in a person. The Holy Spirit "generated" or "regenerated" faith in the first place.

Let's move on to another biblical word, *regeneration*. It refers to an "awakening" or a "becoming aware" process by the activity of the Holy Spirit. Titus 3:5-7 speaks about this: ". . . he saved us. It was not because of any good deeds that we ourselves had done, but because of his own mercy that he saved us, through the Holy Spirit, who gives us new birth and new life [regeneration] by washing us. God poured out the Holy Spirit abundantly on us through Jesus Christ our Savior, so that by his grace we might be put right with God [justified] and come into possession of the eternal life we hope for" (TEV).

Regeneration, then, is when people are "grasped by God," that is, they become aware of a Higher Power in their lives and begin to trust in that Power to maintain sobriety one day at a time.

What all this means is that regeneration began back in Step Two (or earlier). Now in Step Five recovering persons come to terms with their utter inability to justify themselves. They must admit to another human being "the exact nature" of their wrongs and, through this step of complete honesty, cease all attempts at self-justification that they depended upon in the past. Previously, they tried to justify themselves in their own minds and to those persons closest to them. They also tried to justify themselves before God. They failed in all of these areas to make themselves right with God and others.

Now in Step Five all the excuses, alibis, rationalizing, and grandiosity have not changed these persons' relationships with God. They are aware that their behavior has not improved their status with God. They need to surrender themselves to God's grace, to accept that they are accepted by God's grace.

The realization that they have been declared "not guilty" (justified) by God through Christ's death on the cross certainly may not happen the moment alcoholics complete their fifth step. Because of the years of living alienated from God, the Holy Spirit continues to lead these people into the meaning of grace. Hopefully that day will come. Sulo K. told of his delayed realization of acceptance:

> I went into treatment the day before Good Friday. I thought a lot about that. . . . In treatment I took a fifth step. It was great. It was a new start, a new beginning. At first I did not tie what I told in the fifth step in with Jesus dying on the cross for me. But at the Good Friday service a year after I had been in treatment, I was so overwhelmed by that service I just cried. . . . When the choir sang, "Crucify him! Crucify him!" it was so great and so moving. I just got caught up in it. Then later that night I came to a prayer vigil at the church. We could spend some time in prayer or reading. I read the Good Friday and Easter story in the Bible. That's when I realized that all the garbage I had said in the fifth step a year ago was gone. It was great to know that Jesus dying on the cross for me really is a gift. There is no way I can express anything except to be grateful. That's the only way I can be—grateful for what he did.

Recall again the verses in the story of the prodigal son. As he ran to meet his father, the father took charge. The father did not condemn his son's behavior or his appearance. He didn't even say, "I forgive you," because he knew his son felt unworthy of forgiveness! Instead the father ran up to him, threw his arms around him, and kissed him! Despite this, shame persisted—for shame runs deep. The son said, "I am not worthy to be called your son; treat me as one of your hired workers." At that moment the son heard some powerful words. Out of sheer grace, the father hollered out, "Get him a new robe, and a ring, and a new pair of shoes! And that fat calf: Butcher it! We're going to have a party!" These were life-giving words. They were words of affirmation. They reminded the son of the status he had always had. They were words of grace! Suddenly all the shame and guilt, carried those many miles throughout life, fell away. As he felt his father's arms around him and as he heard these words of grace, he recognized a feeling he had never known before. He was accepted! He was forgiven! He was *free!*

As said previously, Step Five, like Step Four, is a step of freedom. It is in the reality of freedom that the bridges of confession, forgiveness, grace, and justification can be appreciated in anyone's walk of faith.

CHAPTER

6

Steps Six
and Seven

*Were entirely ready to have God remove
all these defects of character.*

Humbly asked Him to remove all our shortcomings.

Recovery Must Be Ongoing

Steps Six and Seven are sometimes referred to as the forgotten steps. Often for people who complete their fifth step in treatment, discharge from treatment is soon to follow. They leave on what is called a "post-treatment high." They have discovered a new life without depending on alcohol, and now their world is beautiful. Now that treatment and Step Five are over, the rest of the steps are forgotten.

However, both the alcoholics and their families soon realize that the removal of alcohol does not solve all problems of living. The relational problems they encountered with others and the personal problems they had within themselves are still present. All that has changed is that alcohol has been removed from their lives. Previously the alcoholic and also his or her family believed that if only this person would stop drinking, all the problems they encountered would be eliminated. What a rude awakening awaits them all!

Steps Six and Seven are significant and vital steps in the sequence. They follow what occurred in Step Five for a reason. Rev. Vernon Johnson, in an interview with me, shared the importance of Steps Six and Seven from his perspective.

> The question I ask after Step Five is, "What now? What comes next?" The typical answer is, "I've got to change myself!" That allows us to enter into one of the great Christian heresies. "Oh, you're going to change yourself, are you?" Then I point out that if they are committed at all to the steps of AA, they have just rewritten Step Six. Rather they must call upon God to remove all these defects of character. This then places them into a relationship with God, reiterating their own powerlessness and their basic need of that relationship in order to survive. There must be a dependent relationship upon my God as I understand him at this point. This then is an unfolding process.

Recovering persons must again recall where their strength lies. They really can never forget it if recovery is to continue. It may be time to look back to Step One and remember the powerlessness that was admitted then. That same powerlessness is still here for Steps Six and Seven and needs to be admitted. We cannot change ourselves; only God can. How we all need to remember that!

May we never forget that alcoholism and other addictions are threefold illnesses: physical, mental, and spiritual. Recovery needs to occur in each of these areas. The power that God offers must be incorporated into each of these facets of life for "wholeness of life" to continue.

Alcoholics must now examine their present attitudes and behavior patterns. Notice that Steps Six and Seven shift to the present, whereas Steps Four and Five looked at the past. This shift can be extremely threatening as people may not want to give up some of these "defects." They have used them for many years to con and manipulate people to do what the alcoholics wanted them to. Now they are to ask to have God change them! These two steps are calling for a radical change in their life-style and attitude. Jan Waltner, a chemical dependency counselor in her own private practice in Cloquet, Minnesota, said: "The important thing is the attitude we have. Our attitude is what will make the difference as we take these steps."

The words "were entirely ready to have God remove all these defects of character" can be stumbling blocks. The "Big Book" says:

> We have emphasized willingness as being indispensable. Are we now ready to let God remove from us all things which we have admitted are objectionable? Can he now take them all—every one? If we still cling to something we will not let go. We ask God to help us be willing.[1]

Can this mean that alcoholics are to become perfect? Hardly. Perfectionism has already caused countless problems in most alcoholics' lives. The goal is not perfection; it is progress. Rev. Phil Hansen, former director of the Chemical Dependency

Rehabilitation Program at Abbott-Northwestern Hospital in Minneapolis, said:

> We are never going to get rid of all our defects of character. We are never going to be perfect on this earth, but we still ask God to remove all of these defects. Now this is not going to happen overnight. We may be able to look back a year from now or five years from now and see that some changes have been made. However, the important thing is that we be in the right frame of mind so that we are ready to have God remove them when he makes us aware of them.

BIBLICAL BRIDGES TO STEPS SIX AND SEVEN

Sanctification: God's Power Working in Us

When we are looking for a biblical word or concept by which a bridge could be built into Steps Six and Seven, we find another "major league" word: *sanctification*. We don't use this word in our everyday language. In fact, we rarely use it even in the church! However, it is a biblical word, scattered throughout the New Testament, the meaning of which I believe we need to continue to preach and teach in our churches. *Sanctification* comes from the word *sanctify*, which means "to make holy." Therefore, sanctification is the process of being made holy. Well, how do we become holy? Most of us don't see ourselves as holy. We don't feel very holy!

Before we do some bridge building, let's look at this word as used in two passages of Scripture. "May

God himself, the God of peace, sanctify you through and through. May your whole spirit, soul and body be kept blameless at the coming of our Lord Jesus Christ. The one who calls you is faithful and he will do it" (1 Thess. 5:23).

Also: "But God chose the foolish things of the world to shame the wise; God chose the weak things of the world to shame the strong. He chose the lowly things of this world and the despised things—and the things that are not—to nullify the things that are, so that no one may boast before him. It is because of him that you are in Christ Jesus, who has become for us wisdom from God—that is, our righteousness, holiness [sanctification] and redemption. Therefore, as it is written: 'Let him who boasts boast of the Lord' " (1 Cor. 1:27-31).

What does all this mean? Again, we go back to the work of God's Holy Spirit. In order for sanctification to occur, God needs to humble us spiritually, "knock the pillars out from under us," so to speak, or let us "hit bottom," to use AA language. We need to be brought to a point in which we know that we are totally dependent upon God and God's grace.

Do we enjoy this? Not at all! There is always a battle within us during this process of sanctification. God needs to bring us again and again and again to "square one," in other words, back to the cross of Christ. At the cross we realize that we cannot boast of how great we are spiritually or of wonderful things we have done for the Lord. At the foot of the cross we see again what God has done for us! All our accomplishments, all our sacrifices, melt away. All the "credits" we think we have built up by good deeds are stripped away. We are like beggars in need of a crust of mercy. Though we previously had prided ourselves on what good people we were, we know deep within that we have not lived up to what we should be.

Who is doing this to us? Are we whipping ourselves because we think it will impress God? Hardly! We just read, "May God himself, the God of peace, sanctify you through and through. . . . and he will do it." God is doing this within us because nothing is to distract us from seeing Christ and his cross. We are not holy by our merits; we are made holy by Christ's holiness. We receive his holiness by believing what he did on the cross for us. God's Spirit even helps us to believe that!

Christ in Me

Another aspect of sanctification bridges into Steps Six and Seven: sanctification is Christ living in me. "I have been crucified with Christ and I no longer live, but Christ lives in me. The life I live in the body, I live by faith in the Son of God, who loved me and gave himself for me" (Gal. 2:20).

Sanctification is not something Christ puts in me. It is Christ himself in me! It is not me trying to imitate Jesus. It is the Holy Spirit making the qualities of Jesus come alive in me. As we read in a previous verse, Jesus is our sanctification. God is always working to have us let go of anything that is unlike Jesus so that the holiness of Jesus may dwell in us. How does God do this? By taking us back to the cross! "Therefore, if anyone is in Christ, he is a new creation; the old has gone, the new has come!" (2 Cor. 5:17).

The danger when speaking about sanctification is to try to measure our spiritual progress. It cannot be measured! This is not a progress in which any of us can look back over the last five years and say, "Look how I have changed! Look at how spiritual I am now!" This spiritual progress is not a conscious happening. In fact, it is at those moments when we feel we are in the depths of helplessness and we have not made any spiritual progress at all that our greatest spiritual progress has been made. God has driven us back to Christ and his cross. Here and only here do we know where our hope rests; it always rests with God.

We know that we live in an imperfect world where the human condition spoken about in Step One is still very present and active. We know that in this lifetime we cannot shed this human condition. The more we strive to live as God's own, the more we realize how utterly dependent we are on God's grace in the cross.

Now how does this bridge into Steps Six and Seven? AA also realizes the impossibility of living a perfect life here in this lifetime. The "Big Book" states this clearly: "The principles we have set down are guides to progress. We claim spiritual progress rather than perfection."[2] Recovering persons are aware that more changes are needed in their lives. Removing alcohol from their lives did not solve everything. They are still plagued with impatience, quick tempers, perfectionism, and lust (that, too!). How can they change all this? Steps Six and Seven address that dilemma: "Were entirely ready to have God remove. . . . Humbly asked Him to remove. . . ." Just as sanctification occurs when God brings us to the cross, Steps Six and Seven can only start when God brings recovering persons back to "the beginning." In other words, it is a returning to powerlessness. It is a return to Steps One, Two, and Three. People in recovery remember once again where their power comes from and who, and only who, can change anything in their lives. Their strength and hope have to lie only in God.

Steps Six and Seven are a returning to "the beginning." Sanctification is a returning to the cross where our Christian faith is anchored, and it is a bridge for communication into these two steps. Both of these steps as well as sanctification speak of spiritual progress. William Hulme, professor of pastoral care at Luther Northwestern Seminary in St. Paul, Minnesota, wrote:

> The wisdom of the Alcoholics Anonymous movement is that its program goes beyond sobriety to spiritual development. Yet in contrast to the tangible nature of sobriety, no twelve steps can be counted upon to produce spiritual development.[3]

AA recognizes that the source of power that changes and transforms individuals is, not the steps themselves, but God. It is his power that persons must rest upon; "by ourselves we can do nothing."[4] The spiritual progress in sanctification and in AA is anything but a nice, smooth, steadily climbing line; it is peaks and valleys. It is the valleys, however, that hold the greater blessings for all of us.

Step Seven does raise questions: "Why should I ask God to remove these shortcomings? Why should I have to ask God at all? God knows my needs and God can change me as God wills. Why ask?"

God wants us to ask! Asking reveals, or opens us up to a relationship with God that we could liken to a trusting child coming to a loving parent. God is ready to remove all our shortcomings but wants us to have that kind of relationship in which we come to him with our needs and expect that he will respond in love. "Ask and it will be given to you," said Jesus, "seek and you will find" (Matt. 7:7).

God's Spirit does respond. The change may not be instant, but through our asking, which is a way of prayer, the Spirit gradually causes the "fruit" of the Spirit to grow. "But the fruit of the Spirit is love, joy, peace, patience, kindness, goodness, faithfulness, gentleness, and self-control. Against such things there is no law" (Gal. 5:22).

When persons complete a fifth step, I often ask, "What are you going to do now?" The answer usually has to do with attending AA meetings or finding a sponsor. My encouragement is that they go on to Steps Six and Seven and continue on the road of recovery. As stated at the onset, these two steps are often the forgotten steps, yet they are very important in one's life of sobriety and recovery. Sanctification, too, is often a forgotten part of our spiritual walk, yet it is vital if we are to live life to its fullest. May that be our goal.

7

Steps Eight and Nine

Made a list of all persons we have harmed and became willing to make amends to them all.

Made direct amends to such people wherever possible, except when to do so would injure them or others.

Restoration of Relationships

The direction of the steps now shifts. Up to this point the steps had caused the recovering person to look inward. Now the direction is outward to other people whom his or her life has touched. These two steps deal now with the restoring of relationships, both past and present.

For all of us, people are a part of our past and will be a part of our future. Our relationships with others affect how we feel about ourselves and God. In order for the quality of life in sobriety to continue, it is now time for people in recovery to repair or restore relationships from the past and the present that have been harmed by their drinking or behavior. These two steps are "how-to" steps for this restoration to occur.

Humility and Making Amends

For most of us it is difficult to admit when we are wrong. It is even more difficult to find people we have hurt and to apologize and sincerely try to make amends. The extent to which recovering persons are able to allow themselves to make amends is largely determined by the degree of humility they possess. Zacchaeus, humbled by the acceptance of Jesus, was moved to make amends to those he had harmed: "Look, Lord! . . . if I have cheated anybody out of anything, I will pay back four times the amount" (Luke 19:8). Jesus then went on to say that because of Zacchaeus's willingness to make amends, salvation (a wholeness of life) had come into his life.

Humility is an essential ingredient in living the AA program. It indicates a mental attitude that is imperative in the process of recovery. The Reverend Gordon Grimm says that "the Twelve Steps are not to lead one to perfection but to humility."

The "Big Book" gives these instructions for the action needed in making amends:

> We have a list of all persons we have harmed and to whom we are willing to make amends. . . . Now we go . . . and repair the damage done in the past. We attempt to sweep away the debris which has accumulated out of our effort to live on self-will and run the show ourselves. If we haven't the will to do this, we ask until it comes. Remember, it was agreed at the beginning we would go to any lengths for victory over alcohol.[1]
>
> Meditation and prayer are necessary in order to make amends. No amends should be made that are not preceded by prayer.[2]

Prayer helps recovering persons keep in mind the purpose of making amends. This is essential for their recovery as they pursue the highest quality of life that all the Twelve Steps combined can give them. Through prayer they can go to make amends in faith that God, who has given them the power to stay sober that day, is now directing and guiding them in what they must say and do at the proper time. It is not only for their own benefit and the benefit of those they have hurt that they need to make amends; they also go believing that they are doing God's will. They have begun to see that the Twelve Steps are a road not only to recovery, but also to spiritual wholeness. In conjunction with this, the "Big Book" states: "Our real purpose is to fit ourselves to be of maximum service to God and the people about us."[3]

BIBLICAL BRIDGES TO
STEPS EIGHT AND NINE

Forgiveness and Making Amends

The Oxford Group taught repeatedly that Christ reconciled humankind to God. It followed, therefore, that a person was to extend this forgiveness to other people. The group stated, "Let a person be right with God, and the love for people will inevitably follow."[4] The Oxford Group emphasized the forgiveness taught in Matthew 5:23-24. They went on to say, "Without forgetfulness and forgiveness, life is choked and poisoned by memories and antipathies."[5] The relationships with one another and with God are interlocked. Before people can have a right relationship with God, they must do all they can to restore broken relationships with those they have harmed.

It was realized by the group, however, that there were instances when making amends was not advised. The question was asked, "Why stir up trouble unless you are in a position to *make amends?*"[6] Each person was to seek God's guidance in order that no further harm be committed by going to an individual at an improper time. The influence of the Oxford Group on Bill W. as he wrote Steps Eight and Nine is obvious.

Recovering alcoholics and others in recovery, in desiring to be of "maximum service to God" and others, go forth to make amends. This involves forgiveness in the sense that they realize they have harmed, angered, or hurt another human being. They go knowing that the people harmed may not forgive them or even give them the opportunity to correct the wrong they have done. They still go because they must do whatever they can to restore damaged relationships or to bring some healing to the person or persons harmed. They begin this step realizing that through the preceding steps, particularly Step Five, they are persons forgiven by God. Being recipients of God's forgiveness, they begin to make amends knowing they are the forgiven ones. God, out of grace, has taken the initiative to love and forgive them of all the past. Now they take the initiative to bring greater wholeness into the life of someone they have hurt. The "Big Book" reads: "It is harder to go to an enemy than to a friend, but we find it much more beneficial to us. We go to him in a helpful and *forgiving spirit,* confessing our former ill-feeling and expressing our regret."[7]

Two aspects of forgiveness, the restoration to wholeness and the removal of guilt through forgiveness, have already been reviewed in Step Five. A third aspect of forgiveness in the New Testament is the removal of barriers between God and human beings as well as between human beings themselves.

For Jesus there is no limit to forgiveness. In Matthew 18:22 Peter is instructed to forgive not once, not seven times, but seventy times seven. This is a rabbinic phrase that means "without limits."

The New Testament makes it implicit that it is impossible to have a right relationship with God if a person does not make the attempt to restore or bring "rightness" into a relationship that has been harmed by his or her actions. In Matthew 5:23-24 we are told that if at the altar, meaning the place of worship, you remember that someone you know has something against you, you need to go to that person and make peace with that individual before you can worship God with a clear conscience. It is interesting that Jesus referred to remembering, at the place of worship, someone outside of that place with whom amends need to be made. It is in the context of worship that we again realize we are the forgiven ones. We are the first forgiven by God's initiative. Therefore, amends made are an expression of that forgiveness already received by the recovering individual.

The Cost of Forgiveness

Forgiveness can be costly. Very often the person to whom amends need to be made is not completely free of fault either. Recovering persons can easily justify their behavior, words, or actions. A woman may say, "I know I hurt him, but he did this to me!" As long as this attitude is held, it is an indication that the person recovering does not want to let go of her own hurt or anger. She does not want to let go of this excuse which she can use in the present or future to justify her past behavior or words.

Making amends is not only a matter of humility in swallowing one's pride; it is remembering that "God has forgiven me, therefore I need to forgive that person whom I harmed of anything he or she did to me!" The cost of forgiveness comes into play not only for the person to whom amends are being made, but very often for the recovering person as well.

The future quality of life of recovering alcoholics rests greatly on Steps Eight and Nine. They cannot evade this responsibility. Not only does making amends restore broken relationships, but it has a tremendous influence in the recovering individual's own self-esteem.

I recall listening to a man in treatment who knew he had to make amends to a family he had never met. While driving intoxicated, he had struck one of their children with his car. The child was severely injured. This man was arrested, jailed, and later sent to treatment. He never met the family, and he vaguely remembered seeing the injured child at the side of the road. Not a day passed when he did not think of this child. With that memory came the overwhelming feeling of guilt.

This man knew he had to go and try to make amends to this family. He dreaded it, but one of his goals was to see them right after he got out of treatment. He and I even talked about the words he would use when he met these parents for the first time.

Over a year later, I again saw this man in treatment. He admitted to me that he had lost the courage to see the parents. The guilt he felt over how he had hurt this entire family continued to weigh heavily upon him. He knew he could do nothing to change or improve the child's health or condition. The feeling of helplessness overcame the desire to make amends. Step Nine was always postponed in his mind for a later date. Three months after treatment he resumed drinking.

Often, making amends may only consist of an apology. Certainly, however, there are amends that need to be more than that. I know a man who repaid borrowed money that was long overdue and a woman who returned shoplifted merchandise, knowing that she may have been prosecuted.

In some situations the offended person or persons will not forgive the one making amends. I grieve over cases when a spouse refuses to forgive the spouse he or she divorced perhaps years ago. Equally painful is a situation where adult children will not forgive their father or mother for pain caused years ago in childhood. I grieve with them also as I listen to the physical and emotional pain they experienced in their early years. Maybe they are not ready to forgive. Maybe they will never forgive. This does not change the value of forgiveness, nor does it change the importance for the recovering person of doing Steps Eight and Nine. The primary purpose is not to be forgiven but to go and make amends. The receiving of forgiveness may fortunately be the consequence of going to make amends, but that may not always be the case.

Recovering alcoholics need to always remember that they are willing to go "to any lengths for victory over alcohol." They are going, not because they must be forgiven, but because they have already been forgiven—by God!

The Bible never minimizes the cost of forgiveness. Countless sacrifices were made in the Old Testament for the pardoning of the people's sins. However, the New Testament reveals God's great cost of forgiveness for all humankind. God sent Jesus to die for the sins of the world. This divine act manifests the all-encompassing love God has for every human being on earth. "God offered him [Jesus] so that by his sacrificial death he should become the means by which people's sins are forgiven" (Rom. 3:25 TEV).

Self-Acceptance

Steps Eight and Nine restore self-esteem as they allow recovering persons to make amends to themselves. When through the all-inclusive forgiveness of God people are accepted by God, they can begin to accept and forgive themselves. Dan N. was able to forgive himself through realizing his forgiveness in Christ. He said:

> I forgave myself in the process of time. There are still things from the past that crop up and I have to think about them strongly. I believe I am forgiven by my God through Jesus Christ. I'm comfortable with my life now. I can't say for sure when I said, "I'm an O.K. guy," but I think it was around my fourth-step inventory.

The First Letter of John reads, "If we confess our sins, he is faithful and just and will forgive us our sins and purify us from all unrighteousness" (1 John 1:9). This is God's promise. Those who have journeyed through the preceding steps, particularly Step

Five, are invited to believe the promise God has made to them. They are forgiven. Through Christ's death on the cross they have been declared not guilty. It is in believing this promise that I am empowered by God to forgive myself and accept myself. Self-acceptance and self-forgiveness are needed before people try to make amends. Without these the potential rejection or anger from the recipients of the amends to those making amends may destroy their self-worth even more and intensify the guilt they already feel.

I have known Pat O. for several years. She shared her need to forgive herself before she made amends:

> I remember the first time I was going to make amends over something that was big to me, and the person I made amends to couldn't even remember it. I was really let down, but then I realized that I really hadn't resolved it within me yet. . . . I got some helpful suggestions from others on how to deal with my guilt. . . . The more I could accept the fact of what I did rather than deny it, the easier it was for me to live with myself. . . . The amends I made after I forgave myself had a lot more meaning for me. . . . Until I really took a look at myself and forgave myself, making amends did not have the value it should have. You just don't make amends to make them and get it over with. They are still there if you haven't forgiven yourself.

Whenever we make amends to someone, whenever we have experienced someone's forgiveness, peace comes into our being. Even if that other individual has not wanted to forgive us, the fact that we have made the attempt to bring reconciliation gives us the feeling of self-worth and self-respect.

The blessing of making amends is well worth the cost.

The benefit of making amends to ourselves and others is in being led by God to a better way of life and a new understanding of love. Again we realize utter dependence on God. We experience powerlessness in letting go of past resentments and hurts. Again we need to ask for the power to change our attitude in order that wholeness of life will continue.

Forgiveness and self-acceptance are aspects of life that all of us need to experience in being God's people. They are bridges by which we can have a greater appreciation for each other and for ourselves.

Step Ten

*Continued to take personal inventory and when
we were wrong promptly admitted it.*

Following through Day by Day

Step Ten is a "follow-through" step. Just as athletes
must follow through in their motion, so alcoholics
must follow through in their program. Step Ten can
be viewed as a plateau in the sense that the first nine
steps are the groundwork of the AA program and
Steps Ten through Twelve are a day-by-day main-
tenance.[1] In Step Ten the recovering person com-
mences to put his or her AA way of life into practical
use.

Step Ten is directing people in recovery to take
frequent inventories of their lives. Whereas Step
Four called for an inventory of one's entire life up
to that point, Step Ten now calls for an inventory
on a day-to-day or week-to-week basis. It is called
a "spot check" in AA. It can be done at any time.
Many AA people do it at the end of the day.

BIBLICAL BRIDGES TO STEP TEN

Grace Gives Freedom

The "Big Book" states in regard to Step Ten: "We have entered the world of the spirit."[2] The Spirit of God is a freeing spirit. Jesus said, "So if the Son sets you free, you will be free indeed" (John 8:36). The apostle Paul wrote that "where the Spirit of the Lord is present, there is freedom" (2 Cor. 3:17 TEV). People in AA have found a freedom they did not possess before. Before sobriety they spent their lives hiding and lying. During those drinking years, they were covering up their own feelings, resentments, insecurities, and sense of failure from everyone around them. The best means by which to hide, even from themselves, was in using alcohol. Now, by God's grace, they are free.

In the past they could not face or admit wrongs because of the underlying feelings of inferiority and inadequacy. Now, through their faith, they accept themselves as they are (they "accept that they are accepted"). They are free to remove their masks of perfectionism and reveal their fears and weaknesses. Before sobriety they had tried to live lives of perfection because they could not face failure and criticism. Now they realize that perfection is never attainable, and they can accept themselves as imperfect. They have been given a freedom they never had in their drinking lives.

Freedom always comes with a price. Lasting freedom from alcohol has its price. For this new life of sobriety to remain and mature, recovering alcoholics must be watchful about what is happening around and within their lives. When their behavior or words have hurt someone else, rather than letting false pride justify what happened or letting resentment build, Step Ten encourages recovering persons to have the freedom to apologize and make amends immediately. This daily inventory reminds them of who they are, what they have been given, and from whom their power comes. It is a small price to pay each day for the new life of sobriety to continue.

Christian freedom is never freedom from responsibility. Whenever there is freedom "from" something, there is also freedom "to" something. The apostle Paul wrote in 1 Corinthians 9:19: "For though I am free from all men, I have made myself a slave to all" (RSV). Recovering people are free *from* the power of alcohol; they are free *to* live in the power of God. They are free *from* having to live a perfect life; they are free *to* admit their faults. They are free *from* carrying resentment; they are free *to* make amends. As recovering individuals daily take inventory, they protect these freedoms because they realize what they are free from and also what they are free to be and to do. As they go through their inventories, they become aware that as old faults are eliminated, new ones appear and old ones reoccur.

There is no step in the AA program that is a better reminder to recovering people that they are continually dependent upon God for their sobriety. They realize daily that this new life they enjoy was not earned by their own efforts. They know they deserve no credit for what they have received. The credit and gratitude go to God who daily supplies the power for that day's sobriety.

Free to *Be* and to *Do*

In Christ a person is free to *be*. Recovering alcoholics are now free of the fear of "being found out." Freedom has allowed a new honesty to emerge that must always be lived and practiced or it will be lost and they will go back to the world of hiding, lying, pretending, and, eventually, drinking.

Freedom also allows a person to *do*. Recovering people are free from questions that haunted the past: "What will people think? What will others say? How will I be accepted?" They now are free to choose what is best for them and their sobriety regardless of the opinions of others. Sobriety, they realize, is a gift given to them, and it must be protected and treasured, for if they return to living to impress others, they return to lives of deceit.

The psalmist wrote, "Search me, O God, and know my heart; test me and know my anxious thoughts" (Ps. 139:23). To be able to take our own inventory is a sign of freedom. To take our inventory on a daily basis is to live in freedom and no longer allow the past to hold us in bondage.

The words of St. Paul are appropriate for this chapter: "Freedom is what we have—Christ has set us free! Stand, then, as free men, and do not allow yourselves to become slaves again" (Gal. 5:1 TEV).

Freedom! What a great word and what a great place for all of us to live. It is a bridge word we can celebrate together!

Baptism

There are many different opinions about baptism. However, whether you were baptized as an infant or as an adult, baptism is a bridge into what is being "lived out" in Step Ten.

Step Ten is meant to be a day-to-day, on-going process of "living out" the new way of life the recovering person has discovered through the Twelve

Steps. Baptized people also are involved in a "living out" of what they have received from God in baptism.

Some recovering persons have never been baptized. Obviously, this bridge is for the benefit of those recovering alcoholics who received baptism at sometime in their lives.

Having baptized scores of babies and several adults, I am well aware that after baptism a person may not continue to live in an awareness of God or faith in God's promise. It may also be that after the baptism of an infant no Christian instruction was received. The parents saw the event of baptism as "the thing to do." However, God is not out of the picture! If I did not believe that, I would baptize far fewer people. The Holy Spirit is always active to bring this baptized individual into a relationship with God and an awareness of God's presence. God will never give up on people regardless of who they are or what they may have done or not done. Alcoholics' behavior, guilt, or rebellion may have alienated them from a belief in God's grace, but God's love for them has not ceased. God has claimed them in baptism. For alcoholics to surrender to their powerlessness and eventually repent of their behavior is evidence of the Holy Spirit's activity in baptism.

Baptism can be a great comfort to the recovering person. It can be a source of strength for him or her to look in the mirror and say, "I am baptized! And because I am baptized, God has promised he will never leave me or forsake me. I am always God's child!" Baptism gives us the identity of who we are and whose we are. Living out our baptism is like an invitation from God to daily leave behind our sins in forgiveness and go forward trusting in God's power. It is a "dying and rising" each day.

Baptism can become a great source of strength, faith, self-acceptance, and self-worth as those in AA daily live Step Ten and daily live in their baptismal relationship with God.

Freedom and baptism are relevant daily for quality living. Both make a bridge into Step Ten over which greater communication and perhaps new understanding can take place.

I conclude this chapter with a meditation from *Twenty-Four Hours a Day.*

> I will start a new life each day. I will put the old mistakes away and start anew each day. God always offers me a fresh start. I will not be burdened or anxious. If God's forgiveness were only for the righteous and those who had not sinned, where would be its need? I believe that God forgives us all of our sins . . . and we should be very grateful.[3]

CHAPTER

9

Step Eleven

*Sought through prayer and meditation to improve our
conscious contact with God as we understood Him, praying
only for knowledge of His will for us and the power to
carry that out.*

The Concept of God Changes

Recovering alcoholics often begin sobriety possess-
ing negative feelings associated with the idea of God
or anything religious. However, as they have gone
through the steps thus far, they have learned that
their sobriety rests on their trust in God as they
understand God. The eleventh step now unashamed-
ly directs recovering people to seek a deeper communion with the God of their understanding.

Many people change their understanding of God
as their recovery progresses. David H. told how his
view of God radically changed:

God made my life miserable when I was young. I
hated him. I believed that God had killed my dad in
a car accident and my sister by suicide. I thought he
could have prevented that from happening. So I hated
him. I despised him. . . . When I began AA I had
to put away the God I knew as a child and trust

108

someone else. . . . I believe the AA program led me to know Christ.

Dan N.'s initial concept of God was the "rescuer" image, a God who was called upon in time of emergency. He shared how this image changed:

I know God hasn't changed, but my concept of God is so much different than what it used to be. . . . The concept of God I have now is not a God who'll get me out of jail, not a God who'll just get me out of scrapes, but a God who cares about everything I do and is active in all I do. . . . The concept of the God I have now is Jesus Christ. I do believe that the Son of God is my Savior, and that's the big difference from where I was before.

I have stated that the steps of the AA program should be taken in order since there is a progression from one step to the next. The benefit received from one step is directly related to how well the previous step was applied. There is a link between Step Eleven and the taking of daily inventory in Step Ten. Taking inventory on a regular basis is of little value if the person does not seek to change those things for his or her life. To earnestly seek God's will and ask for God's power to make the necessary changes in one's life is a continuation from where Step Ten left off.

Seeking God's will through prayer and meditation requires disciplining oneself to set aside time for these each day. Recall that the Oxford Group Movement stressed that each member devote some part of each day for a "quiet time," and they believed that early morning was best since it was easier to claim as one's own. After that the day belonged to other people, and it was almost impossible to find a quiet moment. How true that still is today!

Step Eleven directs those in AA and Twelve-Step groups to have some quiet time each day for meditation and prayer. Recovering alcoholics need to focus on their relationship with God and their dependence upon God's power to maintain sobriety. In the past these people had taken every problem or distressful situation to the bottle, but they have now received the power from God to live a radically new way of life. However, sobriety must be lived one day at a time, and the loss of it is only one drink away.

After treatment alcoholics may be filled with excitement and inspiration. The danger that may arise shortly is that this excitement will evaporate and be replaced by disillusionment and depression. Step Eleven is a time set aside each day to remind themselves that they are powerless and that their power to stay sober that day will come from God.

The Oxford Group taught that God had a plan for each person. The person taking Step Eleven realizes that it was God's plan that he or she become sober. Now it is to ask for daily guidance throughout sobriety so that God's long-range plan for his or her life can be completed one day at a time.

I have spoken to people who have been in AA for years who every morning faithfully set aside some quiet time when they can meditate, pray, and read. They are unashamed to say that the quality of their sobriety depends upon this time spent alone with God. Their discipline is a witness to all of us.

I have also spoken to those who, having had a relapse and returned to treatment, say that two things happened before they started drinking again: they stopped attending AA meetings and they stopped asking God daily for the strength to stay sober. The "Big Book" reads: "We constantly remind ourselves that we are no longer running the show, humbly saying to ourselves many times a day 'Thy will be done!' We are then in much less danger of excitement, fear, anger, worry, self-pity, or foolish decisions."[1]

I know that in my own personal life, when I do not take some quiet time each day for prayer, reading, and reflection, I sense that something is missing. If I neglect my quiet time for a number of days, I can feel myself "running out of gas" spiritually. My "tank is going dry." Prayer and meditation are essential for my spiritual energy.

BIBLICAL BRIDGES TO STEP ELEVEN

Meditation

"I meditate on your precepts and consider your ways. . . . Let me understand the teaching of your precepts; then I will meditate on your wonders" (Ps. 119:15, 27).

Meditation means active contemplation. It is not a time of wondering, thinking, or daydreaming. Meaningful meditation depends on purposeful concentration of the mind on a certain subject. It also involves expelling all distracting thoughts and images. I like the way one man described meditation to me. He said, "Imagine in your mind a blank wall with nothing on it. Then let God put whatever words or images God wants on the wall."

Meditation takes practice. It takes discipline of time. Rev. Vernon Bittner says that it is an art:

> Meditation is reflecting and creatively responding to God. There is no scientific method to this approach. Meditation is allowing the mind of God to break in upon us. . . . Meditation can be thinking and reflecting on God's word (or some other writing) and neither debating nor rejecting what God has to say to us. It is resting quietly and allowing God to speak to us through his words. . . . Meditation cannot be imposed or forced. It is being relaxed enough to breath deeply the grace and will of God. . . . We need to begin with our goal in mind—to be in relationship with God. . . . Yet meditation must be "free"; otherwise it is not meditation.[2]

Prayer

Inseparable from meditation is prayer. Prayer in both the Old and New Testaments has many forms. It is encouraged at all times, places, and situations. The apostle Paul wrote, "Pray at all times" (1 Thess. 5:17 TEV). Prayer is seen as the "life blood" in a person's relationship and harmony with God.

Prayer for all of us can take many forms. It can be offered in any place. I recall one late night when an AA member and I were driving a man to a detox/treatment center. This man was just ending a week-long drunk. The AA member was driving, I was by the other front door, and our passenger sat between us. We had driven only a mile out of town when he shouted, "I'm sick. Stop the car!" I had an instant vision of what could happen in this car and all over me! The driver slammed on the brakes. In a split second I had the door open and our passenger was out of the car, on his hands and knees in the ditch, vomiting, or trying to. He finally staggered to his feet, looked up into the dark sky and cried, "God help me!" Three short words, spoken in an unusual place, from a surrendered heart. It was a prayer! He didn't bargain or make promises. He just cried for help. The last I heard, some years later, this man was still sober, living his program one day at a time.

I have found that people in AA talk very freely about prayer. They see it as essential for their sobriety and their spirituality. They do not look upon prayer as some formal, structured speech before God that only a few ordained people are called upon to do. They see prayer, rather, as the intimate communication of their inner being with their Higher Power. Here they are able to share concerns ranging from those of great magnitude to the most trivial. For many, their prayers have changed over the years.

Dan N. told of how his prayer requests changed before and after sobriety began: "I remember times when I was in jail and I would pray, 'Get me out of this one, God, and I won't do it again!' . . . Now my prayers are for guidance and thanks. I try to keep it as simple as I can."

Perhaps one of the greatest rewards or results of prayer is the sense of belonging to God. Most recovering alcoholics struggled with a feeling of isolation and loneliness in their drinking days. Now they realize they are no longer lost and without purpose, because they can have a relationship with God. God is viewed by this stage of the AA program as a God of compassion, concern, and mercy.

"Teach me to do your will, for you are my God; may your good Spirit lead me on level ground" (Ps. 143:10).

This step instructs its members to pray for God's will. Knowing God's will is often a complex task. Frequently the individual's ambitions may get confused with God's intentions. The "12 X 12" states, however, that the thoughts that are not from God will prove to be no answer at all.[3]

Persons practicing the eleventh step hopefully will learn this great biblical truth: when people completely let go of their goals and ambitions, often caused by their own egos, God will direct their lives and, in God's own time, reveal his will for them. Here again we confront the activity of the Holy Spirit, for it is God's Spirit within an individual who is drawing, calling, and leading that person in the ways and will of God (Rom. 8:16, 26; 1 Cor. 3:16; Gal. 5:25).

Worship

People in recovery, as they begin to attend AA meetings, discover a fellowship of people they never imagined could exist. There they meet people with whom they can identify. All of them have carried a similar burden—alcoholism. There they find a concern and understanding they have never encountered in their lives. Previously they believed they were exceptions. They all thought they were the only one who felt the way they did. No one could possibly be like them! Now in this meeting room, they discover they were wrong. The people there have felt at one time the same way the newcomers did. They have come into a community, a fellowship, a communion of people with a special bond: they have been released from a slavery to which they were bound.

There is another fellowship in which many recovering people have also found understanding, concern, love, and support—the fellowship of Christian believers, the church. This is different from the fellowship of AA and rightly so. The AA meeting is not a church, and it is not meant to be. AA is a fellowship of people who believe that a Power greater than themselves has restored them to sanity and to a life of sobriety. The church is a fellowship of people who believe that Jesus Christ has restored them from sin and to eternal life.

Many people who enter AA balk at the suggestion of attending worship. Many argue with me about it. They may have negative feelings about anything related to church and worship. However, it is my conviction that worship completes one's recovery program. The steps of AA begin to restore persons to wholeness and wellness, but, in my opinion, it is an incomplete program because it needs to include a savior. There must be some means by which people receive expiation for their mistakes and shortcomings, which the Bible calls sin. God needs to become humanly involved and known to them through flesh and blood.

About nine years ago I heard Don B. speak at a "Keep It Simple" weekend at Camp Vermilion, a Bible camp near Cook, Minnesota. I share a portion of his taped message since it relates to what I am describing.

> I had been in AA for five years. I was sober. I was living the steps. I had what I was supposed to have, but inside of me there was something missing. There was still an empty space, a void. I had been a Catholic in my younger years. Since I began drinking I had

left the church. Guilt had driven me away. I don't remember how I came to this realization, but one day I decided I wanted to go back to my church, so I did. The emptiness left. What I needed in my life was Christ. I needed a savior. I needed someone who could take all my garbage away, and I realized that Christ did this on the cross. I still go to AA. I also attend church. Christ made my program complete. He made my life complete.

Through the encouragement of people within the church and by the activity of the Spirit of God within this community of believers, recovering people begin to become aware that the living Christ they meet in their AA friends can also be met in those in the church. Worship can strengthen and deepen their conscious contact with God through the hearing of God's Word, sharing in the sacraments, and fellowshiping with other believers.

I will be the first to admit that if we in the church sincerely want people from the AA community to worship in our churches, we have to make some changes in our attitudes and maybe in offering some different opportunities in worship. I asked these two questions of all the people I interviewed: What contributions do you see AA making to the church? What contributions do you see the church making to AA? I share the three following responses.

From Earl H., a recovering alcoholic and a pastor:

What the church can learn from AA is acceptance, openness, the lack of judgmental attitude. . . . All this is healing in an unusual sort of way. I think that is what the church intends to convey, but the message doesn't get through to too many people. AA can serve as a reminder to the church that the church is also to be a caring community.

Dave H. shared what he saw the church needing to do and also what his church had given him:

> I think our church services should be more informal and allow opportunities for sharing . . . the church can give understanding. AA is not meant to be a Christian organization. God gave us AA to get people sober. The church can help people come to know God through Jesus. I was not a whole person until I came to know Jesus Christ as Lord and Savior. . . . That's what the church can give to AA, that wholeness.

From Sulo K., who had not been active in a church before but took membership classes and now sings in his church choir:

> The church and AA gave me a complete program or way of living. . . . I know I need the church. I need God in my life, I know that. For me the church and AA are compatible programs. They work together. I received from the church what I needed in my spiritual life. I need to come here for my spirituality. . . . Alcoholism has a stigma, and I believe that the congregation should become more aware of the disease of alcoholism so the alcoholics in our church could be more accepted by others. . . . The church needs to open its heart to the alcoholic and say, "Come on in! We love you!"

Prayer, meditation, and worship are bridge words and actions we can all use as we strive to grow in our conscious contact with God and seek God's will for our lives. No matter who we are, no matter what we struggle with, may our spiritual quest continue one day at a time.

10

Step Twelve

Having had a spiritual awakening as a result of these steps, we tried to carry this message to alcoholics, and to practice these principles in all our affairs.

Reaching Out to Others

The first eleven steps are primarily concerned with the recovering individuals themselves and their dependency on a Power greater than themselves for sobriety. Step Twelve takes those in recovery beyond themselves to the world around them.

We may hear the expression of someone "going out on a twelfth-step call." As we carefully read this step, it is obvious that there is more to it than merely helping another human being. I will move quickly into the biblical ties I see in this step.

BIBLICAL BRIDGES TO STEP TWELVE

Spiritual Awakening

There are as many variations of spiritual awakening as there are people. There are also perhaps as many different definitions of what a spiritual awakening is as there are people who have had them. However, certainly each one of them has something in common with all the others, as the "12 X 12" points out:

> When a man or woman has a spiritual awakening, the most important meaning of it is that he has now become able to do, feel, and believe that which he could not do before on his unaided strength and resources alone. He has been granted a gift which amounts to a new state of consciousness and being. He has been set on a path which tells him he is really going somewhere, that life is not a dead end, not something to be endured or mastered. In a real sense he has been transformed because he has laid hold of a source of strength which, in one way or another, he had hitherto denied himself.[1]

The apostle Paul wrote, "Do not conform outwardly to the standards of this world, but let God transform you inwardly by a complete change of your mind" (Rom. 12:2 TEV). A transformation, or "awakening," has occurred in the lives of AA people. Their lives have been changed or transformed because they have become aware of a source of Power they had never known before.

These opening words in Step Twelve may imply that a spiritual awakening is something that has occurred in the past and is now over. It is important for us to realize that such an awakening is a never-ending process. It is the result of the Spirit's constant work in our lives. It began in the past, back at Step One, perhaps even before Step One, but it continues on for the rest of our lives.

The apostle Paul alluded to this process when he wrote: "You have put off the old self with its habits and have put on the new self. This is the new being which God, its creator, is constantly renewing in his own image, in order to bring you to a full knowledge of himself. As a result, there is no longer any distinction between Gentiles and Jews . . . but Christ is all, Christ is in all" (Col. 3:9-11 TEV). Paul was writing about the change or transformation the Spirit has caused and is causing within us. The Spirit is still slowly, gradually changing us if we are open and receptive to God. We could say that we are always in the process of "becoming."

The activity of the Spirit is to bring out the person or nature of Christ within us. Paul wrote in Colossians 1:27, "And the secret is this: Christ is in you" (TEV). Through the Holy Spirit's efforts we are becoming reflections of Jesus who is in us. Using the language of Martin Luther, we are becoming "little Christs" to those around us. In Ephesians 4:13-15, Paul used such expressions as "We shall become mature people, reaching to the very height of Christ's full stature. . . . we must grow up in every way to Christ" (TEV). These words reflect an on-going process, or "becoming."

Step Twelve reads, "Having had a spiritual awakening as a result of these steps." Recall how throughout the steps those in recovery had to return continuously to Step One and remind themselves that they were powerless and totally dependent on God. Spiritual awakening began then, too, even though they may not have been conscious that it was a spiritual awakening.

For Christians, a spiritual awakening is received by continuously being brought by God back to the cross of Christ. With a repentant heart they know that they are utterly dependent on God's grace through the cross of Christ. In both AA and the church, one's spiritual life is renewed or awakened by going back to the beginning (Step One for AA and the cross of Christ for the church).

Evangelism

Carrying the message to others is the heart of the twelfth step. This step is important to the recovering person for two reasons. First, as people share their stories, others may admit their own powerlessness and desire help. Second, when twelfth-step people are sharing their stories, it is a strengthening event in their own sobriety. There is value in the giving of ourselves and our own experience. This brings us to an obvious and extremely important bridge with the Bible.

The command of Jesus was to go forth into all the world and make disciples (Matt. 28:19). He also instructed his followers that they were to be witnesses for him (Acts 1:8). We, as followers of Christ, are "message carriers." The lifeblood of the church and indeed every Christian is to somehow be involved in sharing the "good news" of Jesus Christ. It is a wonderful message, for it is a message that brings life out of death, hope out of despair, and joy out of sorrow. It is a freeing message that releases an individual from the bondage of sin and restores that person to a healthy relationship with God.

God has shared himself with the human family by the incarnation of flesh and blood. God's story is a story of people touched by his grace and changed by his power. Every Christian, when sharing the Good News of Jesus with another human being, can also share from his or her own personal story or life because God has moved in different ways with each human being who believes. Evangelism, then, becomes the sharing of God's story in our lives. It is meant to be just that, a "sharing" without pressure, without coercion. It is done in faith that the Holy Spirit will cause the seed that is planted to sprout and bear fruit.

Twelfth-step work is the sharing of a story, the sharing of a gift. Jesus said, "Freely you have received, freely give" (Matt. 10:8). This is the core of Step Twelve.[2] When a recovering alcoholic goes out to share with an alcoholic in need, he or she is the "symbol of hope" in flesh and blood. This is an incarnational event: one human being sharing with another that there is power to be released from bondage.

> Practically every AA member declares that no satisfaction has been deeper and no joy greater than in a twelfth step job well done. To watch the eyes of men and women open with wonder as they move from darkness to light, to see their lives quickly fill with new purpose and meaning, to see whole families reassembled, to see the alcoholic outcast received back into his community in full citizenship, and above all to watch these people awaken to the presence of a loving God in their lives—these things are the substance of what we receive as we carry AA's message to the next alcoholic.[3]

No single group in my experience as a pastor has revealed more zeal and determination to share the message of hope than an AA member going to someone who may need to hear the message. Rev. Vernon Johnson said in a taped interview, "It is the missionary conviction. The gift I have, I have received, and I have a need to share it."

As a pastor I have called upon AA members to visit with someone about whom I, or a relative, was concerned. They never hesitated to go, and not just because it would strengthen their own sobriety. I believe they went because they sincerely wanted that person to become sober. They really desired him or her to have the new life of sobriety they had received.

I remember an AA man whom I will call John. He told me that during a worship service he felt convicted to go to the home of a man he knew. John knew this man had been drinking for days. He knew that if this man continued to drink at this pace he would die. When John arrived at the man's residence, he found the man in his garage, very sick, very shaky. The time was ripe for this man to listen. John simply shared his story of what his life was like before and how it was now. The man listened. He said: "I'm ready to go. Will you take me?" As John told me what happened, he simply called it "God's perfect timing," and he was privileged to be a part of it.

The members of AA see their mission as going forth to plant the seeds of hope. The "Big Book" reads:

> Your job now is to be at the place where you may be of maximum helpfulness to others, so never hesitate to go anywhere if you can be helpful. You should not hesitate to visit the most sordid spot on earth on such an errand. Keep on the firing line of life with these motives and God will keep you unharmed.[4]

Those in AA view their program as a program of attraction rather than promotion. If someone, hearing of the recovering person's story of spiritual awakening, decides to admit his or her powerlessness, that is good. The recovering person rejoices with him or her. However, the person carrying the message knows he or she did not make that person sober. If the hearer stops drinking, it is the result of God's power, and all credit is to go to God.

The Daily Walk

In the words ". . . and to practice these principles in all our affairs," "these principles" means the Twelve Steps and "affairs" means all aspects of one's daily life. The Twelve-Step program has been referred to previously as a way of life. It has done more than simply help people stop drinking; it has begun to restore new life to their total being. As they gain more sobriety, they begin to realize that it is not just alcohol or drugs over which they are powerless. They see that they are also powerless over such things as their spouses, children, friends, and colleagues at work. They begin to realize that they have no control over others' behavior, thoughts, attitudes, or feelings. They cannot make other people do or say or feel what they want. Again they must admit powerlessness. Again they need to pray, "God, grant me the serenity to accept the things I cannot change, courage to change the things I can, and wisdom to know the difference." Great freedom is received from this prayer. It is a freedom that those in recovery find daily in allowing God to guide their lives. "If we live by the Spirit, let us also walk by the Spirit" (Gal. 5:25 RSV).

Gratitude

Sobriety leads to gratefulness. As stated above, recovering alcoholics know that their sobriety is a gift from God. It has been the result of God's power, for they are powerless. In the past they saw only what they could accomplish, whether it be done through money, work, or deceit. Now all of life is a gift that they have been given. They are free to express appreciation to God, to their families, and to others.

One recovering alcoholic in my parish said, "I can never pay God back for what he gave me. I owe everything to God. All I can do is be grateful to God every day and never forget how life used to be."

Rev. Phil Hansen realizes how important one's attitude is in the process of recovery. He said, "If you are grateful for your sobriety, you will probably stay sober; if you are proud of it, you will probably drink again."[5] "There but for the grace of God go I" is not a trite statement to people in recovery. It is a constant reminder that the new life they have received is a gift from God. From the depth of their being they are eternally grateful for God's grace.

The following meditations are from *Twenty-Four Hours a Day*. Both express the necessity of gratitude.

> I will never forget to say thank you to God, even on the grayest days. My attitude will be one of humility and gratitude. Saying thank you to God is a daily practice that is absolutely necessary. If a day is not one of thankfulness, the practice has to be repeated until it becomes so. Gratitude is a necessity for those who seek to live a better life. . . .[6]

> "Praise the Lord." What does praising God mean? It means being grateful for all the wonderful things in the universe and for all the blessings in your life. So praise God by being grateful and humble. Praise of this kind has more power to vanquish evil than

has mere resignation. The truly grateful and humble person who is always praising God is not tempted to do wrong. You will have a feeling of security because you know that fundamentally all is well. So look to God and praise Him.[7]

Thanksgiving and praise are words frequently found scattered throughout Scripture. The psalms are a rich source of expressions of thanksgiving and gratitude that recovering persons may find speak to their struggles and victories. "Give thanks to the Lord, for he is good; his love endures forever. Let the redeemed of the Lord say this—those he redeemed from the hand of the foe" (Ps. 107:1-2).

Stewardship

It is the very nature of God to give, and in grace the best was given to the world. Stewardship is the generous sharing of God's gifts. Paul writes, "For Christ's love compels us, because we are convinced that one died for all, and therefore all died. And he died for all, that those who live should no longer live for themselves but for him who died for them and was raised again" (2 Cor. 5:14-15).

Earlier in his First Letter to the Corinthians, Paul wrote: "This is how one should regard us, as servants of Christ, and stewards of the mysteries of God. Moreover it is required of stewards that they be found trustworthy" (1 Cor. 4:1-2 RSV).

Those in recovery know the meaning of "gift." Their new life, freed from the bondage of addiction, is a gift. Rev. Vernon Johnson said in a personal interview, "The gift I have, I have received, and I have a need to share it. It is through sharing it that

I keep it. It isn't mine to keep; it was given to me."
It is in the twelfth step, biblically speaking, that
recovering people become stewards in sharing the
portion they received through God's grace and God's
mysterious ways. If stewards keep their portion for
themselves, they lose it; if they give it to others, the
portion increases. This truth the recovering person
learns in Step Twelve.

It is important to the sobriety of people in AA to
tell others about their surrender and gift. It is by
telling or teaching others that they grow stronger in
their own sobriety. When they share how life "used
to be," they realize to an even greater degree what
they have been given. By telling his or her "story,"
each person becomes even more grateful. Dan N.
told how strength was received through telling others:

> You really get stronger when you reach out and
> help someone and they take that hand and something
> positive happens. You gain strength from the neg-
> ative reactions, too, because you realize you don't
> want to be back in the puke. That's not where you
> want to return. It's a constant reminder.

Discipleship: The Disciplined Life

Christianity is a way of life. Early Christians were
called the people of "the Way" (Acts 9:2). Life in
Christ is freedom in Christ. It is living in the grace
of God, knowing at all times that we are claimed by
God in baptism and that each day is a block of time
to live in relationship with and for God. It is resting
back in the joy and serenity that Christ can give as
we confront everyday issues and traumatic events.

As Christians, we, too, are powerless over many facets of our lives, but we trust in him who has all power.

The Christian way is a life-style directed and guided by a Power greater than ourselves whom we know as the God revealed in Jesus Christ. It is a journey of faith, trusting that Jesus called us to be his and also calls us to a purpose beyond ourselves. To this great purpose of sharing God's story and ours with others, we are sent out stumbling, broken, imperfect people, yet made whole by God. We are the disciples, the message bearers, God's own people, that we may declare the wonderful deeds of a God who called us out of darkness into marvelous light. We are disciples, for we are disciplined by God's grace and forgiveness. The Twelve Steps are also a discipline, a discipline that also leads to freedom.

A wise man once said, "Only the disciplined are free." How true that is for everyone. *Only* the disciplined are truly *free*.

Afterword

AA and the Church

That open meeting in Rugby, North Dakota, seems like a long time ago. Because of people and events God has sent into my life, I am not the same person I was then. However, my opinions about the fellowship of AA have not changed since I "discovered" this group that night above the florist's shop. It is a great community of caring people who know that by the grace of God and the Twelve Steps they have received a new life. They talk about it. They celebrate it. They want to share it.

I continue to be inspired, fascinated, and spiritually recharged as I listen to AA speakers at open meetings. I still find my heart touched as I listen to the stories of men and women transformed by the power of God. I know miracles do happen.

That is not to say that I have not been inspired and renewed at a worship service or in witnessing the lives of people in the church, because I definitely have been. I have seen and received love, understanding, encouragement, and acceptance from these people. My life has been blessed by this caring community called the church. Here, too, I have seen miracles and lives transformed.

There are distinctions between AA and the church as we all know. These need to be recognized. Although there are similarities that both may discuss at great length, they certainly are not identical. AA is not a religion. AA was established to be a program by which alcoholics could become sober and live a radically different life-style through the power of One greater than themselves.

Although AA and the church are not one and the same, it is my contention that the two complement each other.

AA is able to offer to recovering alcoholics something the church cannot completely give, namely a fellowship of people who completely understand their own struggle with alcoholism and surround each other with acceptance and support. This does not mean that those in the church do not understand the struggles associated with fallen humanity. Each person there is also affected by the human condition. However, not everyone in the church understands alcoholism. Many see it simply as a moral weakness, saying things like, "Those drunks could stop drinking if they would just set their minds to it!" Unfortunately society's view of the alcoholic as a weak, undisciplined, worthless creature may often be carried into the church, although the extent of that stigma's influence in a church depends on the congregation and the community it serves.

In turn, the church is able to give to recovering alcoholics what AA cannot, namely, the faith in a God who has been revealed in a human being. No longer do recovering persons have to attempt to conceptualize a vague, nebulous "Higher Power." They can know God and God's saving grace through Jesus Christ and Christ's sacrificial love. No longer do alcoholics need to question or wonder about God's forgiveness. Through the cross they are cleared of all sin and guilt. This does not mean that there are no Christians in AA who do not share their faith, for some openly tell of their faith in Christ. However, AA cannot and does not endorse any religion, Christian or non-Christian. The church's gift, then, is to aid the recovering person's progress in his or her belief in a Higher Power to a loving God who became a human being in Jesus Christ for the salvation of the world.

I believe that AA and the church have much to offer each other. There needs to be more sharing and understanding of how God has brought healing and wholeness into our broken lives. This is happening in some communities and in some churches. It must happen more often. We need to get beyond seeing people as "those sinful drunks" or those "hypocrites." We are all children of God who have strayed, who are in need of grace, and who have been saved by a loving God.

I believe we have a common bond out of which communication, understanding, and acceptance can occur. That bond is a Book that inspired Dr. Frank Buchman to begin the Oxford Group Movement, which ultimately touched Bill W. and Dr. Bob. It is the same Book that the Christian church teaches and preaches from every week. This Book tells the story of God's saving grace for all people. It is from the Bible, the Word of God, that bridges can be built and God's people can celebrate together.

Two Roads

AA and the church are parallel roads, traveling the same direction, covering similar terrain, yet consistently maintaining their distance. Although both have a great concern for human life, they view life around them through different glasses. AA limits its concern to this life; the message of the church is about life on both sides of death. AA acknowledges that all humans are imperfect and that some are in bondage to alcoholism; Christianity claims that all people have fallen short of the glory of God and are in the bondage of sin. AA declares that men and women need a Power greater than themselves to restore order and sanity in their lives; Christianity claims that God has revealed himself in a human being, Jesus Christ, and changes people's lives by the power of the Holy Spirit. AA speaks of forgiving oneself and leaving the past behind; Christianity proclaims forgiveness through Christ who removes the past from us. AA speaks of a Higher Power; Christianity speaks of a God who desires to be known personally.

Though there are differences in these parallel roads, there are places along the way where both AA and the Christian church have some common ground. This is so evident that no one has to search for hidden themes upon which both may converse. The common ground is in the words *grace, message, power,* and *change* (transformation).

Both AA and the church proclaim the grace of God. The men and women in AA know that their sobriety rests upon God's grace. A seminary professor said to his class, "If you want to know about grace, go talk to an alcoholic." Every day of living without a drink, recovering alcoholics know, is a gift from God which they have done nothing to deserve, earn, or merit. It has been given to them, and they have received it.

Both AA and the church have a message to share. Everyone in AA has a story to tell of how God, as they know God, has given them a new life. Church members have stories to tell as well, of how God has come in Christ and how God has come to them in a subtle or dramatic way.

Both AA and the church believe in a God of power. God is not stationary in either AA or the church. God is a God who acts to help people do what previously they could not do alone.

Both AA and the church know that lives can be changed. God works in mysterious ways his wonders to perform. Those who work with alcoholism see lives transformed before their eyes. This change can be given many names, but it is still change. A person is not the same person he or she was a year ago or a week ago or an hour ago. For such individuals, something beyond their own power has entered which before had been excluded. They are new creations. They have been changed, and they will continue to be changed throughout life.

The two roads will never merge into one, but if bridges can be built between the two, if communication can begin with similar beliefs and convictions, even though spoken in different terminology, then both may grow richer, stronger, and more cooperative in their caring for the human family.

Hopefully, as the years pass, more bridges, wider and stronger, will be built. Upon them may we all journey back and forth, gaining from each other. May we all press on, learning to live in greater harmony with our God, ourselves, and our neighbors.

It is in this harmony that we find acceptance and freedom and receive the life God intends for all of us.

In this harmony AA and the church can come to appreciate each other's program or ministry to suffering people. Then there can be a sharing of treasure. "Yet we who have this spiritual treasure are like common clay pots, in order to show that the supreme power belongs to God, not to us" (2 Cor. 4:7 TEV).

Our lives are fragile like clay pots. Yet God has made alive and available grace and power beyond ourselves for all of us to experience. May we share this treasure we have received with those we meet on the roads and bridges of our lives. Because we have met, because we have come to know and understand each other, may we all grow.

Notes

Foreword

1. *Alcoholics Anonymous Comes of Age: A Brief History of A.A.* (New York: Alcoholics Anonymous World Services, Inc., 1957), 261.
2. Ibid., 269.

Chapter 1

1. *Alcoholics Anonymous Comes of Age: A Brief History of A.A.* (New York: Alcoholics Anonymous World Services, Inc., 1957), 53.
2. *Alcoholics Anonymous*, 3d ed. (New York: Alcoholics Anonymous World Services, Inc., 1976), 11.
3. Robert Thomsen, *Bill W.* (New York: Harper & Row, 1975), 221.
4. *Alcoholics Anonymous Comes of Age*, 63.
5. Ibid.
6. Ibid.
7. Ibid., 67.
8. Ibid.
9. *Dr. Bob and the Good Old Timers* (New York: Alcoholics Anonymous World Services, Inc., 1980), 96.
10. *Alcoholics Anonymous Comes of Age*, 161.

Chapter 2

1. *Alcoholics Anonymous* (New York: Alcoholics Anonymous World Services, Inc., 1976), 58-59.
2. John E. Keller, *Ministering to Alcoholics* (Minneapolis: Augsburg Publishing House, 1966), 3.

3. *Lutheran Book of Worship* (Minneapolis: Augsburg Publishing House, 1978), 56.
4. *Twenty-Four Hours a Day* (Center City, Minn.: Hazelden Foundation, Inc., 1975), meditation for October 7.
5. Harry M. Tiebout, "The Ego Factors in Surrender in Alcoholism," *Quarterly Journal of Studies on Alcoholism* 15 (1954): 11.
6. *Alcoholics Anonymous,* 11.
7. Ibid., 45. Emphasis mine.

Chapter 3

1. *Twenty-Four Hours a Day* (Center City, Minn.: Hazelden Foundation, Inc., 1975), meditation for June 9.
2. John E. Keller, *Ministering to Alcoholics* (Minneapolis: Augsburg Publishing House, 1966), 3. Emphasis mine.
3. *Alcoholics Anonymous* (New York: Alcoholics Anonymous World Services, Inc., 1976), 51.
4. Ibid., 55.
5. Ibid., 57.
6. Martin Luther, "Small Catechism," *The Book of Concord,* ed. Theodore G. Tappert (Philadelphia: Muhlenberg Press, 1959), 345.
7. *Alcoholics Anonymous,* 25.
8. Ibid., 45.
9. *Alcoholics Anonymous Comes of Age: A Brief History of A.A.* (New York: Alcoholics Anonymous World Services, Inc., 1957), 64.

Chapter 4

1. *Twelve Steps and Twelve Traditions* (New York: Alcoholics Anonymous World Services, Inc., 1952), 46.
2. *Alcoholics Anonymous* (New York: Alcoholics Anonymous World Services, Inc., 1976), 64.

Chapter 5

1. *Alcoholics Anonymous* (New York: Alcoholics Anonymous World Services, Inc., 1976), 73-74.
2. *Twelve Steps and Twelve Traditions* (New York: Alcoholics Anonymous World Services, Inc., 1952), 57.

3. Ibid., 58.
4. *Twelve Steps and Twelve Traditions*, 58-59.

Chapter 6

1. *Alcoholics Anonymous* (New York: Alcoholics Anonymous World Services, Inc., 1976), 76.
2. *Alcoholics Anonymous*, 60.
3. William Hulme, *The Dynamics of Sanctification* (Minneapolis: Augsburg Publishing House, 1966), 131.
4. *Alcoholics Anonymous*, 64.

Chapter 7

1. *Alcoholics Anonymous* (New York: Alcoholics Anonymous World Services, Inc., 1976), 77.
2. *An Interpretation of the Twelve Steps of the Alcoholics Anonymous Program* (Minneapolis: Coll-Webb Co., 1946), 78.
3. *Alcoholics Anonymous*, 77.
4. Irving C. Benson, *The Eight Points of the Oxford Group* (London: Oxford University Press, 1936), 30.
5. Ibid., 33.
6. Ibid., 41. Italics mine.
7. *Alcoholics Anonymous*, 77. Italics mine.

Chapter 8

1. Philip Hansen, "Step Ten," *The Twelve Steps with Phil Hansen*, cassette series.
2. *Alcoholics Anonymous* (New York: Alcoholics Anonymous World Services, Inc., 1976), 84.
3. *Twenty-Four Hours a Day* (Center City, Minn.: Hazelden Foundation, Inc., 1975), meditation for February 1.

Chapter 9

1. *Alcoholics Anonymous* (New York: Alcoholics Anonymous World Services, Inc., 1976), 87-88.
2. Vernon Bittner, *You Can Help with Your Healing* (Minneapolis: Augsburg Publishing House, 1979), 121.
3. *Twelve Steps and Twelve Traditions* (New York: Alcoholics Anonymous World Services, Inc., 1952), 106.

Chapter 10

1. *Twelve Steps and Twelve Traditions* (New York: Alcoholics Anonymous World Services, Inc., 1952), 110.
2. Ibid., 114.
3. Ibid., 113.
4. *Alcoholics Anonymous* (New York: Alcoholics Anonymous World Services, Inc., 1976), 102.
5. Philip Hansen, *The Twelve Steps with Phil Hansen*, cassette series, tape 1.
6. *Twenty-Four Hours a Day* (Center City, Minn.: Hazelden Foundation, Inc., 1975), meditation for January 22.
7. Ibid., meditation for May 30.

For Further Reading

BOOKS

Alcoholics Anonymous, 3d edition. New York: Alcoholics Anonymous World Services, Inc., 1976.

Alcoholics Anonymous Comes of Age: A Brief History of A.A. New York: Alcoholics Anonymous World Services, Inc., 1957.

Arthur H. *The Grieving Indian: An Ojibway Indian Shares His Discovery of Help and Hope*. Winnipeg: Intertribal Christian Communications (Canada), Inc., 1988.

Benson, C. Irving. *The Eight Points of the Oxford Group*. London: Oxford University Press, 1936.

Bittner, Vernon J. *You Can Help with Your Healing*. Minneapolis: Augsburg Publishing House, 1979.

Church, F. Forrester and Terrence J. Mulry. *One Prayer at a Time: A Twelve-Step Anthology for Those in Recovery and All Who Seek a Deeper Faith*. New York: Collier Books, Macmillan, 1989.

Dr. Bob and the Good Old Timers. New York: Alcoholics Anonymous World Services, Inc., 1980.

Hansen, Philip L. *Alcoholism: The Tragedy of Abundance*. Minneapolis: Park Printing, Inc., 1982.

_____ . *Sick and Tired of Being Sick and Tired*. Lake Mills, Iowa: Graphic, 1971.

Hulme, William E. *The Dynamics of Sanctification*. Minneapolis: Augsburg Publishing House, 1966.

An Interpretation of the Twelve Steps of the Alcoholics Anonymous Program. Minneapolis: Coll-Webb Company, 1946.

James, William. *The Varieties of Religious Experience*. New York: Collier Books, 1961.

Johnson, Vernon. *I'll Quit Tomorrow*. Revised edition. New York: Harper & Row, 1980.

Keller, John E. *Alcohol: A Family Affair*. Santa Ynez, Calif.: The Kroc Foundation, 1977.

––––––– . *Let Go, Let God*. Minneapolis: Augsburg Publishing House, 1985.

––––––– . *Ministering to the Alcoholic*. Minneapolis: Augsburg Publishing House, 1966.

Kurtz, Ernest. *Not-God: A History of Alcoholics Anonymous*. Center City, Minn.: Hazelden Educational Services, 1979.

Oates, Wayne. *Alcohol In and Out of the Church*. Nashville: Broadman Press, 1966.

Shoemaker, Samuel M. *The Conversion of the Church*. New York: Fleming H. Revell Co., 1932.

Stewart, David A. *Thirst for Freedom*. Toronto: Musson, 1960.

Taylor, G. Aiken. *A Sober Faith*. New York: Macmillan, 1953.

Twelve Steps and Twelve Traditions. New York: Alcoholics Anonymous World Services, Inc., 1964.

Twenty-Four Hours a Day. Center City, Minn.: Hazelden Foundation, Inc., 1975.

HAZELDEN FOUNDATION "STEP" PAMPHLETS

Published in Center City, Minnesota

Jensen, James G. *Another Look at Step One*. 1972.
––––––– . *Step 2, A Promise of Hope*. 1980.

_____ . *Step 3, Turning It Over*. 1980

Kellerman, Joseph L. *AA—A Family Affair*. n.d.

_____ . *Alcoholism: A Merry-Go-Round Named Denial*. 1969.

Mel B. *Step 10, A Good Tenth Step*. 1982.

_____ . *Step 11, Maintaining the New Way of Life*. 1982.

Pat M. *Step 8, Restoring Relationships*. 1982.

_____ . Step 9, *Making Amends*. 1982.

Sellner, Edward C. *Step 5, A Guide to Reconciliation*. 1981.

Springborn, William. *Step One: The Foundation of Recovery*. 1978.

Step 4: A New Fourth Step Guide. 1974.

Step 5: And the Truth Will Set You Free. 1983.

Step 6: Getting Ready to Let Go. 1983.

Step 7: Let Go and Let God. 1983.

Step 8: Getting Honest. 1983.

Step 9: Building Bridges. 1983.

Step 12: The Language of the Heart. 1983.

OTHER PAMPHLETS

A Clergyman Asks About Alcoholics Anonymous. New York: Alcoholics Anonymous World Services, Inc., 1961.

Today Is Different . . . Than Yesterday. Minneapolis: Johnson Institute, 1976.